The Non-Philosophy Project

Essays by François Laruelle

Gabriel Alkon and Boris Gunjevic, editors

Telos Press Publishing
New York

Printed in the United States of America
16 15 14 13 12 1 2 3 4 5

ISBN: 978-0-914386-47-6

Library of Congress Cataloging-in-Publication Data

Laruelle, François.
Non-philosophy project : essays / by François Laruelle ;
Gabriel Alkon and Boris Gunjevic, editors.
p. cm.
ISBN 978-0-914386-47-6
1. Philosophy, Modern. I. Alkon, Gabriel. II. Gunjevic, Boris, 1972- III. Title.
B791.L35 2012
190--dc23
2011052159

Telos Press Publishing
431 East 12th Street
New York, NY 10009

www.telospress.com

Contents

A Note on the Texts in this Volume

In the mostly occasional essays and interventions presented here, Laruelle introduces non-philosophy to the philosophically sophisticated reader. The introductions are either general and programmatic (as in chapters one and five) or by way of constructive polemic intended to establish a new and non-philosophical usage of philosophical discourse. Two of the polemics are aimed at particular philosophers: against Deleuze, chapter two attempts to distinguish between immanence as virtual (and thus given to philosophy in its opposition to the actual), and immanence as real identity, radically foreclosed from philosophical thought; against Derrida, chapter three attempts to distinguish meta-philosophy, by which philosophy tries and fails to grasp itself by projecting itself as its own other, from transcendental science, which takes philosophy as unilaterally given (without-givenness) according to its ultimate identity in-One.

Polemical in different ways, the other essays in this volume take particular philosophical materials, in the form of common terms and concepts, as occasions for positing an ultimate identity or radical immanence that separates these materials from their common meaning and usage. Chapter four criticizes philosophy's conception of itself as a special and universally translatable language, every utterance of which is susceptible to recursive interpretation and re-translation; instead Laruelle proposes an irreversible translation from the philosophical—a unilateral translation, by suspension, of philosophical recursions according to the axiom of radical immanence. Chapter six focuses on the contemporary philosophy of the event, the concept by which philosophy attempts to engage with what most immediately disrupts its own coherence. The entire structure of the philosophical event, Laruelle argues, is determined in advance by the philosophical decision presupposing the world as given by knowable transcendentals; the supposed event is nothing other than the replacement of the world by these transcendentals hypostatized—the philosophical moment par-excellence. Philosophical materialism, every bit as abstract as the idealism to which it is ostensibly opposed, is the target of chapter seven. And chapter nine takes up related material provided by the philosophical ideas of practice and efficacy. The standard question about the effects of thought, Laruelle argues, is typically philosophical in its duplicity: it presumes that thought can know in advance its own effects, that it can step outside of itself to know what it is doing even as this is being done. Non-philosophical thought does not propose to know its effects, as if these could be objectively grasped; it knows only the effect of real immanence in and through the particular worldly and philosophical materials with which this immanence is ultimately identical.

In the background of both chapters seven and nine is the figure of Marx, whose concept of determination-in-the-last-instance is the explicit subject of chapter eight. The attempt by Marx (and then Engels and Althusser) to conceptualize immanent determination is the closest precedent of Laruelle's project. The factor ultimately determining the immanent process in its totality is, for Marxism, the economic conflict between the means and forces of production. By contrast Laruelle argues that the ultimate immanent determinant cannot be distinguished from immanence as a determinant, from the radically given immanence of the One. Determination-in-the-last-instance must be unilateral and therefore foreclosed from thought. There can be no going back from or interpretation of the determination that *is* real identity.

GA, BG

Acknowledgments

For permission to reproduce materials that first appeared in other venues, the editors and publisher are grateful to the following:

> *Pli: The Warwick Journal of Philosophy*, for chapters 1, 2, 6, and 7;
>
> Hong Kong University Press, for chapter 4, which appeared in *Traces* 4: *Translation, Biopolitics, and Colonial Difference*, eds. Naoki Sakai and Jon Solomon (2006), 55-72;
>
> Presses Universitaires de France, for chapter 8, which appeared in French as the third chapter of *Introduction au non-marxisme* (2000), 39-55;
>
> Taylor and Francis, for chapter 9, which appeared in *Angelaki: Journal of the Theoretical Humanities* 8.2 (2003), 169-189.

Further bibliographical information is provided at the start of each chapter.

The editors would like to thank François Laruelle for supporting this project intellectually and logistically. In addition we would like to thank Ray Brassier for his assistance and his writing, which has greatly facilitated our encounter with Laruelle's work. And we are grateful to Tim Luke, Marie Piccone, Allie Simmons, and the staff of the Telos Press, whose patience, skill, and encouragement have helped bring this project to fruition.

The author himself would like to give special thanks to Ray Brassier and Boris Gunjevic, to whom he dedicates the publication of this volume.

Introduction

According to the Identity of the Real: The Non-Philosophical Thought of Immanence

Meta-Philosophy, or Philosophical Self-Presupposition

Francois Laruelle is the contemporary thinker who has most trenchantly criticized the self-presupposing and circular character of even the most apparently "advanced" philosophy. Modern philosophy after Kant has ostentatiously criticized the power of thought to grasp its object. But according to Laruelle, the post-Kantian claim to discern the limits of philosophical knowledge, to set philosophy against an inaccessible other, actually perpetuates and aggrandizes traditional philosophical pretenses: setting the real beyond or against philosophy is nonetheless to define it in philosophical terms—to presuppose a (negative) adequation between philosophy and the object it cannot reach. Philosophy objectifies its ostensible other by reducing it to a negative term in its own discourse. The "end of philosophy" announced by Nietzsche and Heidegger has, Laruelle observes, taken the form of a proliferation of specifically philosophical accounts of the difference between thought and what it would know. These supposedly self-critical philosophies are in fact insidious exaltations of philosophy's power to know its own limitations and to preemptively incorporate all forms of extra-philosophical thought. The quintessential "lie" of modern philosophy is its claim to admit that it is "lying," to describe and account for its own intrinsic failures and limitations. In doing so philosophy simultaneously posits

its other and brings it within the scope of its own discourse. The inadequacy of philosophy is what modern philosophy uniquely knows—and so it presumes to know what it does not and cannot know. Only in the absence of this presumption, Laruelle contends, is it possible to discern the limitations of philosophical discourse and thereby to apprehend its true form, its actual way of knowing.[1]

The presupposition of the adequacy of thought to the real defines philosophy as such. The presupposition is the same whether the real is defined in advance as the known or as the unknown—the latter definition merely reducing the real to the negative correlate of the philosophical concept. Thought undertaken in the absence of this presupposition is, by Laruelle's definition, "non-philosophy." The inaugurating postulate of non-philosophy is that thought is in no way other than the real; the relation of thought and the real cannot, therefore, be understood as a relation of adequation or of inadequation. In his discourse the non-philosophical subject cannot objectify the relation (or non-relation) of reality to thought. But for Laruelle the de-objectification of knowledge does not preclude the possibility of a specifically non-philosophical way of knowing.

The modern emphasis on the difference of philosophy from what it would know is, on Laruelle's account, fundamentally

1. The author who has done the most to bring Laruelle to the attention of the English-speaking world is Ray Brassier. The account of Laruelle in this introduction has benefited from Brassier's presentation of Laruelle's project in his essay "Axiomatic Heresy: The Non-Philosophy of Francois Laruelle," *Radical Philosophy* 121 (2003), 24-35. Also see Brassier's book *Nihil Unbound: Enlightenment and Extinction* (Houndmills: Palgrave Macmillan, 2007), 118-49. Another important account of Laruelle's project appears in John Mullarkey's *Post-Continental Philosophy: An Outline* (London and New York: Continuum, 2006), 125-56.

consistent with the meta-philosophical ambition that has characterized philosophy from its pre-Socratic beginnings. Philosophy has always tried to get outside itself so as to know itself by accounting for its own possibility—the possibility of its systematic relation to the extra-philosophical. The intrinsic meta-philosophical ambition of philosophy seems impossible to fulfill: to conceptualize its relation to its other, philosophy would have somehow to know itself and its other apart from that very relation. Thought and being would have to be known in themselves, apart from each other, if the actual constitution of their relation were somehow to be known or even imagined. But there is no thought without the actual thinking of things other than thought. And there is no way thought could ever access matter, or world, or being, in a putatively pristine unthought state. Thought cannot know what it knows without knowing it—and so thought cannot transcend its own relativity so as to grasp it as a unity.

The impossibility of finally closing upon itself in a secure unity of subject and object has not, however, thwarted philosophy in its meta-philosophical ambition. It has rather served as the preeminent occasion for philosophical claims of self-knowledge: for in recognizing its difference from what it knows, philosophy has, since Parmenides, identified itself with this very difference—as a transcendentally given differential relation. Philosophy, according to Laruelle, is the claimed identity-in-difference of thought and being, of philosophy with what is not philosophy. When the emphasis is on the overcoming of difference in identity, as it has been for much of the philosophical tradition, the overcoming is still defined in differential terms—as the identity of elements given as distinct (thought and being, mind and matter, concept and intuition), an identity that can only be comprehended philosophically. In this structure philosophy is one of the elements within the differential relation (thought or mind assimilated to philosophy) and simultaneously the identity of the differing elements (the comprehension of philosophy and its other meta-philosophically). At once inside and outside of the relation, philosophy looks at itself and its other as a commensurable pair, as distinct entities that are implicitly correlated even in their difference, and thus philosophy is able to treat the relation abstractly, as a single object for thought. Even though a full unity with its other is impossible, this impossibility is itself reduced to a unified object—difference as transcendentally given, as itself an identity.

The Differential Identity of Modern Philosophy

The circular pattern is most evident in post-Kantian thought. For Kant the posited inaccessibility of the thing-in-itself makes necessary the transcendental deduction of the possibility of the object's assimilation to thought, through intuition, schematization, and categorization. Crucially, the assimilation can never quite be accounted for—the crossing can be divided into ever finer layers of mediation—and this conceptual ramification *is* Kant's philosophy. The assimilation cannot be accounted for, and yet it is in fact presupposed from the beginning—for what else does philosophy explain? In his late works Kant himself realized that his entire project had depended upon the presupposed correlation of the unknowable with the mechanisms of knowledge; all along, in other words, he had understood difference as a relation. His idealist inheritors took this correlation or differential relation as the object of their explicit speculation. Laruelle's non-philosophy is an attempt to think without presupposing this correlation, without assuming that thought is somehow related in difference to what is not thought.

The difficulty of this undertaking became evident for Laruelle during his study in the 1970's and 1980's of Heidegger, Nietzsche, Derrida, and Deleuze, the modern "philosophers of difference" whose works, Laruelle contends, betray the same self-presupposing structure of earlier philosophies.[2] Though they no longer emphasize the overcoming of difference in the identity of differential relation, these thinkers still subject difference to conceptual identification, and implicitly exalt philosophy as the place where the transcendental truth or givenness of difference (or virtuality, or will-to-power) is exposed. Thus for Deleuze the power of self-differentiation functions in the "plane of immanence" as a kind of absolute that perpetually instantiates and disrupts the forms of discrete actuality; and it is philosophy that discerns the truth of difference, the dynamic power of the immanent differential process, in the movement to and from particular actualities. Philosophy is actual, but it also knows the differential relation of the virtual and the actual; it is inside and outside of itself. As Laruelle contends in the second chapter of the present volume, Deleuze's positing of a planar and virtual immanence sets it as a kind of background or "field of presence" correlated to the philosophical subject, who knows actual objects in their emergence from and return to the immanent process that is their implicit precondition.

In some respects Laruelle is closer to Derrida, who does not associate difference with immanent forces but rather with the cognitive structure of recognition and self-recognition. In

2. Laruelle presents his conclusions about these authors in *Les philosophies de la différence. Introduction critique* (Paris: PUF, 1986). This work has recently been published in English translation as *Philosophies of Difference: A Critical Introduction to Non-Philosophy*, tr. Rocco Gangle (London and New York: Continuum, 2011).

Derrida's account the subject forever differs from itself because its identity depends on self-apprehension, intrinsic to which is the space of self-difference that renders full self-comprehension impossible. Only its own alterity as object allows the philosophical subject to know and identify itself—but this self-identification is as such a self-division and a falling away from or exceeding of itself. This understanding of alterity, according to Laruelle's arguments in the third chapter of this book, still presupposes it as "sufficient or absolute," which means that it is correlative, if only negatively, to the subject that it simultaneously constitutes and disrupts. The subject is still the privileged site for the manifestation of difference, which is given in the subject as its own internal fissure or intrinsic impossibility. Difference can still be conceptually grasped by the philosophical subject who describes his own self-division. By setting it against the philosophical aspiration to identity, deconstruction defines difference in philosophical terms—as the frustration/object of its desire—and thereby hypostatizes difference and makes it graspable conceptually. Deconstruction has not relinquished meta-philosophical ambition, for the identity that it places beyond self-differing philosophy is still defined in terms of the frustration of meta-philosophical desire, the impossibility of self-closure.

The Event as Philosophical Decision

In the sixth chapter of this book, Laruelle uses recent philosophical accounts of "the event," which are supposed to concern what is beyond philosophy, to show with special clarity the way in which philosophy is unable to escape the presumption of its own sufficiency. The concept of the event in Derrida, Deleuze and other thinkers following Nietzsche and Heidegger, is deployed so as to manifest in philosophy what is ostensibly beyond it. This manifestation involves the disruption of a realm of thought understood as relative and limited, an ontic realm subjected to continuous and consistent reference (associated by Laruelle with the relative transcendence of knowledge about being, knowledge as *meta-*). Philosophy allows for the disruption of this mode of thought in the emergence or breaking-in of its other—which may be either a deeper unity that dissolves discrete appearances (the true One as Other) or a more irreconcilably transcendent Other. The event is the vertical impingement, as from another level of reality, of an unconditioned beyond (*epekeina*) upon the realm of consistently knowable forms of apparent being. The philosophical thinking of the two levels, *meta* and *epekeina*, is enabled by the manipulation of opposed pairs of hypostatized transcendental terms—the One, the Other, Multiplicity, Being-as-such. The ontic or actual level is conceived as a "hybrid" or combination of opposed transcendental terms—the Multiple and the One, for example, resulting in conditioned multiplicity; or Being and particular form, resulting in discrete being. In the event the hybrid forms of being are eliminated or attenuated in favor of the purified extreme terms, which are immediately unified or brought into conflict. Instead of being discretely combined, as they are in relative and visible forms, the transcendental terms fuse, interpenetrate, flow, or erupt. The event is the thought of the unthinkable in the posited identity of opposed terms; the best example of this pattern is provided by Deleuze's account of the event as the perpetual excess of self-differentiating power over given actualities, or as the ceaseless virtual act by which actual forms are dissolved and recomposed, or as the accession of diverse forces to the oneness of pure multiplicity in the endless flight between conditioned multiples.

What makes this general approach to the event philosophical is the way the two realms—of conditioned and unconditioned, relative and absolute—are thought in terms of each other. The transcendental terms are hybridized to account for the appearance of discrete and knowable beings; the same terms are polarized and fused to evoke the event that transcends and transforms these beings. The *epekeina* and the *meta*, the relative and the absolute, form a single philosophical system—they are posited together and are mutually presupposed. Not only is the event known through its effects on the conditioned realm; the very notion of conditioned being presupposes the possibility of the event that undoes it. The event is in fact an effect of the philosophical understanding of reality as split into two levels, one of which is supposed to give the other through a process of conditioning or differential relation. The notion of particular being as the combination of opposed transcendental terms (whether of One and Multiple, or Being and One, or Being and Other) already holds the possibility of the identification of opposed terms that is the event.

According to Laruelle, the true event for philosophy is in fact the coordinated positing of relative and absolute, combined and separate, conditioned and unconditioned, as mutual presuppositions—there is no event apart from the philosophical "decision" that sets these oppositions in motion. This decision is the "proto-event," which is the self-positing of philosophy as the discourse concerning the relation of the unconditioned to what it conditions, or of the transcendental to the given. This relation, which becomes an immediate unity in the event, is the presupposition that establishes philosophy's adequacy to its other. The presumed correlation of actual being to a transcendental conditioning power is what allows philosophy to know itself through the other by moving beyond the other as given. It is the sheer being-given of what it knows that philosophy must resist; its skill is the derivation of the transcendental—the transcendental that is its unacknowledged presupposition. The event, which undoes the given in the immediate presence of its preconditions, is the true culmination of philosophy—the moment at which it need no longer depend on its objects, which are replaced by the transcendentals that are the preserve of philosophy alone.

Presupposed by Thought: The Real Transcendental

The philosophical circle can only be broken by real knowledge of philosophy, which has to arrive at its object from outside the circle of self-presupposition. This non-philosophical knowledge must allow itself to be determined by its object—philosophy as such—from which it has to remain separate; in this sense non-philosophy must be like positive science. But the subject of non-philosophy cannot simply be identical to the scientific subject. If non-philosophical knowledge is to do more than negate philosophy as an illusion, then it cannot abandon the transcendental aspect of philosophical discourse. Non-philosophy must, Laruelle insists, be transcendental in the sense that it must concern the way reality is given to thought. For philosophy this givenness can always be grasped *through* the given—for the object is presupposed as given through a conditioning or differentiating process that is the *same* as that which differentially relates the subject to its object. Philosophy knows the object by knowing its own difference from (and relation to) the object. This knowledge always entails philosophy's reflexive self-discovery because the philosophical decision on the real as transcendentally given or conditioned *is* the self-positing of the philosophical subject as that which knows or derives this conditioning. To know philosophy objectively and non-philosophically requires the suspension of the subjective self-constitution of philosophy in the transcendental circle of conditioning and conditioned, or givenness and being-given.

As the object of non-philosophical knowledge, however, philosophy must still be seen as given, for it must appear to a subject. But it must be seen as given-without-givenness—and not as given by a process of conditioning or individuation that can be known through what it gives. The subject of non-philosophy can no longer presume that the given has been given *to him*; he must accept the given as present without any derivable process of donation.

What is given, what is radically immanent in and *as* philosophy, is the mode of transcendental knowledge in which it operates. To know this mode of knowledge, to know it without entering into its circle, is to practice a science of the transcendental, the "transcendental science" of non-philosophy. This science is *of* the transcendental, but according to Laruelle, it must also itself *be* transcendental—it must be a global theory of the givenness of the real. A non-philosophical transcendental is required if philosophy as a whole, including its transcendental structure, is to be received and known as it is. Philosophical knowledge may be "hallucinatory," but this hallucinatory knowledge remains a real phenomenon. To dispel an illusion is not to know it; to know it requires that it be known according to its actual givenness—the determination or conditioning by which it really comes to appear. Philosophy must then be known as it is given—as it is transcendentally determined or conditioned—but somehow this knowledge must avoid lapsing into the philosophical derivation of a presupposed conditioning power through the object that it ostensibly conditions. The real transcendental determination of philosophy cannot be philosophically derivable. The non-philosophical subject must therefore know philosophy according to a transcendental that is radically foreclosed from philosophy—though for this very reason it is its real determination or transcendental cause.

This cause cannot, in Laruelle's view, be a presupposition of non-philosophy, for presuppositions are accessible through what they effectively condition and are therefore material for philosophy. What non-philosophy requires is rather the transcendental reality that is *presupposed* by all thought—a presupposed reality that cannot be derived as the condition of any particular thought, object, event, or phenomenon. If it is presupposed *by* thought, then the transcendental cannot be derived from anything given *to* thought—and so it cannot be articulated in the form of an otherwise implicit presupposition. The reality presupposed by thought—if it is really transcendental, if it is really presupposed—cannot be an object of thought. What is presupposed by thought cannot be a thinkable presupposition. But though this foreclosed reality cannot be an object of thought, it is not entirely inaccessible to thought. It can still be accessed by a form of thought that follows the exigencies of this foreclosure. The foreclosure demands that thought accept that it can never take what it presupposes as its own object—for the presupposed is not other than thought but rather is radically *immanent* in and as thought. The form of thought, according to Laruelle, that accepts and accords with this immanence—the immanence of the foreclosed transcendental—is the un-derived axiom. The positing of this axiom—the axiom of thought's immanent identity to the real—is the beginning of non-philosophy.

Immanence Is Identity: The Axiom According to the One

With this primary axiom non-philosophy suspends the presupposition by which thought is differentially related to its other—the presupposition that allows philosophy to identify itself as the thought of this difference. For non-philosophy thought is instead radically and unthinkably identical to what it would think. This identity is not coincidence, synthesis or truthful correspondence; it is identity "in-the-last-instance," to use the crucial phrase Laruelle adapts from Marx—the identity of thought and what it would think insofar as both are seen according to "the One," according to the unthinkable reality of radical immanence.

As Laruelle understands it, immanence is sheer identity; there can be no immanence "to" anything else, for this sets immanence in relation to something other than itself—to some form of exteriority or transcendence. Though the "immanence to self" that defines Deleuze's virtual plane of immanence is meant to be distinguished from immanence to any determinate whole, the "to" gives the plane a self-consistency that correlates it to the philosophical subject, who relates discrete actualities to the immanent forces by which they are singularized and dispersed. For Deleuze immanent virtuality is still given to the subject, not within the stability of the actual but as the dynamic differential relation that destabilizes and virtualizes the actual (see, again, chapter two). By contrast Laruelle posits radical immanence as an identity which precludes all relation because there can be no distance from it. There is no other to this identity, not even a transiently discrete actuality that would ultimately be dissolved by it. Such discrete forms of course exist, but they are already identical to and in the One. The subject and the things it discerns are identically immanent—not "to" anything but insofar as they are real at all. The immanence of the real simply cannot be seen or known—not as the other to thought, not as the differential relation of thought to this otherness. Thought itself is real, is immanent, and can never be otherwise.[3]

3. In his recent work Laruelle has been hesitant to apply the term "identity" to the radical immanence of the One. Instead he has used the term "superposition," borrowed from the theory of quantum mechanics. Objects

On this point Laruelle's notion of immanence can also be distinguished from that of Michel Henry, though the two share important similarities. Like Laruelle's immanence, the immanent auto-affection posited by Henry is foreclosed to thought; but Henry also *opposes* the self-closure of pure auto-affection to the alienation of thought, whereas Laruelle sees thought and everything else as identical in radical immanence. It is precisely because thought *is* immanent that immanence cannot be subjected to thought. The failure of philosophy to accept this—to accept that it cannot know itself in its immanent identity—is the reason why philosophy cannot know itself at all. The foreclosure of immanence to thought is in fact the transcendental determinant of philosophy as such, which is nothing other than the attempt to overcome this foreclosure by positing it as otherness or as differential relation. True alterity, according to Laruelle, is not otherness but the identity of immanence "in the flesh." This reality is not beyond philosophy; it is foreclosed to philosophy because it *is* philosophy—it is the act or force that is thought "in-person," a force that is identical in-the-last-instance to the immanent force of everything "in-One."

The radical identity of the non-philosophical One allows for no exterior and thus no interior. It lacks all consistency, but neither is there anything apart from it with which it could be called inconsistent—it is without-consistency, just as it is

---

seen according to the One are "superposed" and not logically identified. For more on the non-philosophical use of quantum theory, see *Philosophie non-standard. Générique, quantique, philo-fiction* (Paris, Kimé: 2010). Despite Laruelle's recent qualifications and modifications, the term "identity" has been essential to his work and is required for any understanding of the non-philosophical project. The term therefore appears throughout this introduction, though readers should be aware that its meaning is determined through its usage.

without-being and without-otherness. Nothing can be separated from it—and so it is separated not only from the notion of separation but also from that of union. There can be no thought about the One, for this implies a pre-existent thinker, separate from the One, who could take up a relation to it—whereas the thinker is always already in-One. Non-philosophical thought "according to the One" must be determined by the One—determined in and *through* its own radical immanence to everything that it is. The One must determine this thought along with the subject capable of thinking it—somehow acting on the subject with which it is identical, exerting its causality upon it through the identity of radical immanence. The non-philosophical subject *is* this thought, which takes the form of the axiomatic postulation of the One itself.

This postulation "accords" with the One by which it is determined, but this determination is without an identifiable determinant. It emerges from no discernible sequence or process. The positing of the One cannot be received as a fact or phenomenon to be interpreted, as if the One were a condition giving evidence of itself through that which it conditions. The One does determine the positing that accords with it, but there is no way back to the One from what it determines. There is no relation *between* the One and the thought or positing of the One; the thought seems to be distinct from, and thus related to, the One, but this relation appears only to thought. From the perspective of the One, the real identity, there is no difference between itself and what it determines. The determination can thus be called "unilateral." As real transcendental, the One is radically foreclosed from the thought with which it accords; it cannot be deduced as presupposition or conditioning process. The immanent identity of the One allows for no movement in thought beyond the thought that posits it—for there is nothing beyond or other than the One, to which the thought is in-the-last-instance identical. Thought cannot grasp this immanence by positing it as differentially related to the actual thought that it already is. Radical immanence is thinkable only according to its unilateral effect as the thought that knows itself as caused by its own immanent and ungraspable identity.

The Stranger-Subject of Non-Philosophy

The question then is what allows the thought to exist as such, to be discrete. With respect to the One, the thought is not discrete—it remains in-One. As the effect of immanent causality, the thought is distinct only with respect to itself. This thought is what Laruelle calls the "experience" of radical identity or of the "vision-in-One." Terms like thought and experience and vision are all potentially misleading insofar as they suggest a pre-existent subject to which the One appears and by which it is known—whereas according to Laruelle the One is knowable only insofar as it immanently causes or determines the subject of non-philosophy. This subject does not "have" an experience of the One; it *is* the experience of the vision-in-One or thought according to the One, the experience of its own immanent causation.

How can the subject experience the causation by which it is? This experience can be related to philosophical notions of subjective experience only in-the-last-instance. This is not the experience of perception and judgment; rather it is the experience of the axiomatic positing of the One that initiates non-philosophical activity. This postulation is an act that is performed by the subject, but it is "performed-without-performance"—for there is no pre-existent subject to which the act can be attributed. The subject is this performance and does not exist otherwise. The subject is given in the act of postulating the One, given in its own self-performance.

Who or what performs the act if there is no pre-existent performer? What gives the act of the subject, if it arrives as given? According to Laruelle the only answer to these questions is the postulation of a reality foreclosed to thought—in other words, the questions force a repetition of the act of axiomatic positing that occasions the questions in the first place. There is no inferential or analytical path back from the given to the source, no derivation of conditions from what is conditioned, for the subject is the thought of its own identity to its cause. What is radically immanent cannot be derived or inferred from the given, for such derivation presumes an attenuation of immanence and the need for (philosophical) actualization.

The postulation of the One is given, but without givenness, without any possible recession into a presupposed realm of virtual conditions; it arrives not from an inferred "hinterland" of givenness but rather from the "u-chronic" and "u-topic" identity of the immanent real. Impossible to correlate with any identifiable cause, the subject of non-philosophical thought arrives as if from nowhere, or as if it were the uncanny arrival of the already-given. Its arrival seems without cause, for it does not extend the network of worldly interrelationships posited by the philosophical subject, which knows itself by knowing itself and the world as interrelated objects of mutual determination or conditioning. According to the vision-in-One, the subject and the objects to which it is differentially related are identical and identically given in real immanence. This leveling vision enacts a causality other than the network of worldly determinations—a causality of immanence that effects the arrival of the subject that sees according to this immanence.

The causality of the One cannot act within the worldly realm, the world in which objects are knowable as discernibly conditioned. Without-being and without-thought, "devoid of ontological, linguistic, and worldly consistency," the One is separated beyond all relation from the object-world. The One can still, however, affect the world from which it is separated, for this separation is the non-relation of immanent identity. The effect of the One can be exerted only through its own immanence. As immanent identity, the One does not give itself as that which conditions or produces the objects of the world; the One remains itself, independent of the world precisely because it is identical to it in-the-last-instance. Seen apart from this identity, the world is an array of dynamically interrelated objects which develop and affect each other in philosophically interpretable processes. But when seen in its radical immanence, the world of philosophy can serve as an occasional cause of the non-philosophical vision-in-One. And in fact for subjects in the world, the vision-in-One must always be occasioned in this way—as the non-intuitive "experience" of philosophical "material" postulated as identical in-the-last-instance to its immanent cause.

The philosophical material is required to effect or "effectuate" the vision-in-One because the One as such (in-One) does not express or represent itself by affecting worldly objects in any visible way. Its manifestation occurs through the One's determination of conditioned objectivity as such—through its effect upon the mode of representation and cognition that objectivity is: philosophy. The One cannot affect philosophy from outside of it, as if philosophy were an object upon which the One could act. Instead the One affects philosophy through immanence, through its identity in-the-last-instance to philosophy's transcendental structure. (This notion of a final and unilateral causality through immanence—the non-philosophical radicalization of Marx's determination-in-the-last-instance—is the basis for the critique in this book's eighth and ninth chapters of philosophical conceptions of practice.) In a sense the effect of real identity changes nothing; the causality of the One leaves no discernible trace on the objects of the philosophy-world. The change is the arrival of the subject of non-philosophy, the subject that is the act of thought performed-without-performance, given-without-givenness, through the radical immanence that it thinks.

This subject, Laruelle says, "is not something facing me." Because it is determined by an ineluctable immanence with which it remains identical, the non-philosophical subject cannot be posed against the particular objects reflected in philosophy by being derived according to its conditions. The "Stranger-subject" of non-philosophy is an unseen face turned towards a faceless future; this face can be "seen" by the subject who, instead of trying to perceive or face it, posits itself as ultimately identical to it. The face of this identity, the surface of this immanence, is not a visible composure; it is formed in the vision that sees everything, including itself, as unilaterally ("uni-facially") given, untraceably and irretrievably—as given entirely to the future.

Cloning: Philosophy and Non-Philosophy

Philosophy gives itself as absolute, self-positing, autonomous. But it is also given according to the One as "relatively autonomous." The "taking into account" of the relative autonomy of philosophy is what the non-philosophical subject "does." The relativity of philosophy's autonomy does not simply negate philosophy or the philosophical subject; the exposure of the illusions perpetuated by its self-presupposing discourse does not mean that philosophy is itself an illusion. Its pretensions do not separate it from the real One. Laruelle insists that the being-given of philosophy does not undo its autonomy, because in the being-given without-givenness of the One, there is no other, no hidden givenness or conditioning process, which can be derived as the "truth" behind or beyond the philosophical given. The identity of radical immanence is foreclosed to philosophy because it cannot be determined as conditioned—but this foreclosure leaves the immanence of philosophy itself intact and autonomous, for there is nowhere other than philosophy to turn for its true reality. This autonomy is nonetheless relativized, for it must be taken as given—a being-given of philosophy that is all the more radical precisely because it cannot be derived as a thinkable givenness.

When seen according to the vision-in-One, the philosophical "material" or "occasion" for non-philosophy is thus "cloned": nothing is changed, philosophy remains its autonomous self, but this autonomy is now "experienced" or posited as given-without-givenness, as identical in-the-last-instance to everything real. Cloning is causality through radical immanence—a causality which by definition can have no discernible effect apart from the immanence that it already is. The effect of immanent causality is the effectuation of the One in the cloning of the philosophical material that is the occasion of non-philosophy. The effectuation of the One affects nothing because everything is already in-One, in the one real identity with no outside, no other, no shape or synthetic structure. To see philosophy and its world as cloned is, according to Laruelle, to receive them as they already are, as given in immanence, and not as the philosophical subject would have them be, as objects through which transcendental presuppositions can be derived. The non-philosophical subject of this reception *is* this reception, which means that the subject is identical to what it receives or takes as given-without-givenness. The subject is what is given; there is nothing else. This is the identity of-the-last-instance, the identity postulated in the u-chronic and u-topic vision in which the philosophy-world and the subject are determined according to the unilaterality of the real.

The cloning of philosophy is what Laruelle calls the "transcendental function" of real immanence, a function effectuated only in the vision-in-One whereby philosophy is brought forth as immanent, as given-without-givenness. In this function the real is the constant, the variable is philosophy in its various forms, and the outcome is the "dualysis" of philosophy and world: the bringing forth or determination of philosophy in-the-last-instance as *both* discretely autonomous *and* identical, without synthesis or unity or combination, to what it thinks—and identical also to the non-philosophical subject that is nothing other than the reception or effectuation of this identity. In-the-last-instance philosophy and what it thinks are distinct but identical as radically immanent or given-without-givenness.

This immanence is itself transcendental, not in the philosophical sense of the unconditioned that is given through what it conditions, but insofar as it is a universal and ineluctable reality foreclosed from thought: everything is already given, as it is, including thought itself—whereas the content of philosophical thought is deduced by being abstracted from this being-given. The real transcendental, as opposed to the philosophical one, is forever foreclosed from what it gives. It is foreclosed from what it gives because it *is* what it gives, which is the identity of the real as being-given without-givenness. Whereas philosophical transcendental terms are given through what they condition and are thus accessible to thought, the real transcendental is radically given and is therefore foreclosed from thought. Thus while philosophy derives its own identity with the transcendental by thinking the givenness of its objects, non-philosophy separates itself from philosophy—and separates philosophy from its objects—by accepting both philosophy and its objects as unthinkably given in immanence.

Advent: The Immanence of the Future

Laruelle claims that non-philosophy separates philosophy from its objects and thereby exposes the object-world to an unknown future. The world is the synthetic combination of philosophy and the objects that it posits as the products of transcendental conditioning and as therefore susceptible to philosophical knowledge. When seen in-One, the philosophy-world is transformed into—or cloned as—"world-thought," which is the non-synthetic identity, the duality-without-division, of thought and its objects. To see thought and its objects in this way, rather than as combined or synthesized, is to see them as separate but at the same time as identical in immanence. The vision-in-One takes the entire philosophical apparatus, the simultaneous identity and difference of thought with its presupposed others, as given-without-givenness—as relatively autonomous with respect to the real from which it is foreclosed and with which it is ultimately identical.

No less, but no more, real than anything else, philosophy is thus leveled with the world that is its object—and according to Laruelle this releases the world from the philosophical presupposition of its conditioned objectivity, its correlative sufficiency for philosophy. The world, in other words, is released from itself, from its structure as world-object. When the world is no longer seen as presupposed by philosophy, as a set of objects knowable as conditioned—when the world-thought combination is cloned as a duality that is ultimately identical, as an identity-without-synthesis—then the entire world has been brought into the unknown reality of the future. In its bringing forth as given-without-givenness the world arrives from no depth or distance—no *meta*, no *epekeina*. There is no process of objectification to analyze, no distance crossed by the given for thought to traverse once again. This arrival is an "advent" that comes from nowhere, that presents again what was already present, but now turned towards and into the invisible face of the Stranger-subject. In this turning the given is itself estranged, for it is identified with the unseen face—the solitary and unilateral face of the future, or of the present as it faces the future for the first time.

In the non-philosophical advent, the release of the philosophy-world from its own self-sufficiency is not the transcendence of this world. The future towards which the world is turned cannot be beyond the given. Whereas the philosophical event perpetually dissolves the given into its preconditions, the advent of the non-philosophical Stranger-subject is also the advent of the world. According to Laruelle, to see the world in-One, to see it as identical to an immanence that cannot be seen, does not dissolve the world but brings it forth in the form of an unthinkably given autonomy. The world is all the more real when its sufficiency for thought, its conditioned objectivity, is suspended—when it can no longer be presupposed as given across a philosophically derivable depth or distance. As it is released and received in the advent of the subject of non-philosophy, the world, says Laruelle, is brought forth as a non-objective reality. The things of the world still exist, but no longer as objects sufficient for philosophy's derivation of its own presuppositions. Instead of being linked to correlative forms or concepts, worldly objects relate to nothing beyond themselves—which is to say that they enter a future that cannot be anticipated according to established patterns of substitutive pseudo-transformation. The advent of the real future can start only with things as they are, as they are given, and not insofar as they can be substituted for each other according to the systemic logic of the world as philosophical object.

Chapter 1

A Summary of Non-Philosophy

Translated by Ray Brassier

The Two Problems of Non-Philosophy

1.1.1. Non-philosophy is a discipline born of reflection upon two problems whose solutions finally coincided. On the one hand, the problem of the One's ontological status within philosophy, which associates it, whether explicitly or not, with being and with the other, but refuses to acknowledge its radical autonomy. On the other hand, the problem of the theoretical status of philosophy, insofar as the latter constitutes a kind of practice, affect, or existence, but one lacking in a rigorous knowledge of itself: philosophy remains a field of objective phenomena that have not yet been subjected to theoretical overview.

1.2.1. Concerning the first point, there follow an observation and a proposal. First the observation: the One is an object at the margins of philosophy, an object of transcendence stated in

This essay was first published in English translation in *Pli: The Warwick Journal of Philosophy* 8 (1999), 138-148. The English text also appeared on the website of the Organisation Non-philosophique Internationale (www.ONPhi.net) in June, 2003. A French version of the essay appeared in Laruelle's book *La lutte et l'utopie à la fin des temps philosophiques* [*Struggle and Utopia in the Endtimes of Philosophy*] (Paris: Kimé, 2004).

terms of the *epekeina* rather than of the *meta*. Accordingly, it is as much other as One, as divisible as it is indivisible; an object of desire rather than of 'science.' It occurs to the thinking that is associated or convertible with being, without being thought in its essence and origin ("How does the One necessarily occur to man-the-philosopher?"). Philosophy establishes itself within being and within a certain 'forgetting of the One' which it continually exploits in the name of being while supposing it as given from the start.

1.2.2. Now the proposal: finally to think the One 'itself,' independently of being and the other, as that which is incommensurable with them and non-determinable by thought and language ('foreclosed' to thought); to think *according* to the One rather than trying to think the One. But to think this non-relation to thought using the traditional means of thought; to think this displacement relative to philosophy with the help of philosophy; to think by means of philosophy that which is no longer commensurate with the compass of philosophy and escapes both its authority and its sufficiency. These are the terms of the new problem.

1.3.1. Concerning the second point, there follow an observation and a proposal. First the observation: philosophy is regulated in accordance with a principle higher than that of reason: the *principle of sufficient philosophy*. The latter expresses philosophy's absolute autonomy, its essence as *self*-positing/donating/naming/deciding/grounding, etc. It ensures philosophy's domination of all regional disciplines and sciences. Ultimately, it articulates philosophy's idealist pretension as that which is able to at least co-determine the most radical real. The obverse of this pretention, the price of this sufficiency, is philosophy's congenital inability to think itself in a manner that would be rigorous, non-circular, and non-question-begging; in other words, that of *theory*. Philosophy is self-reflection, self-consciousness; it thinks or, in the best of cases, feels itself thinking when it thinks; this is its cogito. Philosophy never proceeds beyond the scope of an enlarged cogito, an immanence limited to self-reflection or self-affection. It is a practice of thought, or a feeling and an affect. As such, philosophy manifests no more than its own *existence* and fails to demonstrate that it is the real to which it lays claim, or that it knows itself as this *pretension*. Implicit in philosophy's existence is a transcendental hallucination of the real, and implicit in philosophical 'self-knowledge' is a transcendental illusion.

1.3.2. Now the proposal: how to go about elaborating, with the help of philosophy and science but independently of the authority of the principle of sufficient philosophy, a rigorous theoretical knowledge, but one that would prove adequate or attuned to philosophical existence, to the philosophical manner of thinking? These are the terms of the new problem.

The Identity of the Problem of Non-Philosophy, or the Solution

2.1.1. The principle of the solution: this is the same thing as positing the One as radically autonomous real with regard to philosophy, but a real thought according to a novel use of philosophy's now reformed means. It is the same thing as making of the One the real condition or cause for a theoretical knowledge of philosophy. The solution constitutes a new problem: how can we, using the ordinary means of thought, conceive of the One as no longer philosophizable or convertible with being, and at the same time as capable of determining an adequate theory of philosophy?

2.1.2. Non-philosophy typically operates in the following way: everything is processed through a duality (of problems) that does not constitute a two or a pair, and through an identity (of problems, and hence of solution) that does not constitute a unity or synthesis. This way is known as that of the 'unilateral duality' which is just as much an 'identity.'

2.1.3. The resolution of the problem requires two transformations which form an identity of transformation. First, the transformation of the philosophical One-Other into a radically autonomous One-in-One; the transformation of the One as object of philosophy into vision-in-One and into a phenomenality capable of determining knowledge.

2.1.4. Second, the transformation of the self-referential usage of philosophical language that regulates the statements of philosophy, into a new usage (both real and transcendental, of identity and of unilateral duality) that furnishes those statements with a double yet identical aspect: at once axiomatic and theorematic. The statements of the One and of its causality as vision-in-One, rather than as object or instance of philosophy, are generated by gradually introducing terms and problems of philosophical extraction, but terms and problems that are now subjected to a usage that is other than philosophical; a usage with a double aspect: axiomatic on one hand, theorematic and thus transcendental on the other; or relating to the real on one hand, and to its effects on philosophical existence on the other.

2.1.5. The One is not an object or entity 'in-itself,' in opposition to a language subsisting 'in-itself,' so as to compose a philosophical or dialectical pairing of opposites. The vision-in-One as matrix of thought is a 'speaking/thinking *according to* the One.' Nor is it a relation of synthesis between the One (i.e. the real) and language. It is a non-relation, a 'unilateral duality.'

2.1.6. All the statements of non-philosophy appear as axiomatic insofar as they constitute the identity (in-the-last-instance) of the unilateral duality, and as transcendental theorems insofar as they constitute the unilateral duality that accompanies this identity. The theorems may serve as axioms on condition of determining-in-the-last-instance other theorems; the axioms may serve as theorems on condition of being determined-in-the-last-instance by other axioms. Axioms and theorems do not constitute two distinct classes of expressions, as they do in science. But neither do they constitute a reciprocal duality of propositions whose donation and demonstration are, certain exceptions aside, ultimately convertible, as they do in philosophy.

From the One to the Vision-in-One

3.1.1. *Immanence.* The One is immanence and is not thinkable on the terrain of transcendence (ecstasy, scission, nothingness, objectivation, alterity, alienation, *meta* or *epekeina*). Corollary: the philosophies of immanence (Spinoza, Deleuze) posit immanence in a transcendent fashion. Even Henry posits in a quasi-transcendent fashion the non-ecstatic immanence he objectifies.

3.1.2. *Radical immanence or immanence (to) itself, the One-in-One.* The One is immanence (to) itself without constituting a point or a plane; without withdrawing or folding back upon itself. It is One-in-One and hence that which can only be found in the One, not with being or the other. It is a *radical* rather than an *absolute* immanence. The 'more' immanence is radical, the 'more' it is universal or gives-in-immanence philosophy itself (the world, etc.).

3.1.3. *Identity, the real and the ego.* The other possible first names for the One are identity, the real or the ego. The One is identity 'in flesh and blood'; the identity that is no longer attribute nor even subject. It is the ego rather than the subject, the latter being determined-in-the-last-instance by the ego. The One is the radical real which 'is' not, not because it could have 'been,' but because it is 'without-being'; the One or the real does not 'exist' but (is) in-One.

3.1.4. *Non-intuitive phenomenality.* The One is vision-in-One. The latter manifests the One alone and manifests it according to the mode of the One. Consequently, it is not a mode of perception; its phenomenal-being falls neither within the purview of perception nor within that of the phenomenological phenomenon. It is without intuitivity in general, either as objective or intellectual intuition, and without thought or concept; it does not think yet it 'gives'...without-givenness. Its radical non-intuitivity allows philosophical terms to be used according to a mode of axiomatic abstraction, but one that is transcendental.

3.1.5. *The given-without-givenness.* The vision-in-One is a mode of being-given that is without-givenness (devoid of any mixture of given and givenness, devoid of any 'backstage' or 'background' givenness, and devoid of any self-giving). It does not give, it is the given, but it is able to give an instance of givenness according to its own mode of being-given, which is neither that of cognition nor that of representation: this is its universality.

3.1.6. *Non-consistency.* Since the One is not beyond (*epekeina*) essence or being but only in-One, it is devoid of ontological, linguistic, and worldly consistency. It is without-being and without-essence, without-language and without-thought, even though it is said to be thus with the help of being, language, and thought, etc. This non-consistency entails that the One is indifferent to or tolerant of any material, any particular doctrinal position whatsoever. It is able to determine the usage of any material so long as the latter possesses the ultimate form of philosophy. This does not mean that the One subsists in-itself, in transcendent isolation, absolutely unrelated to language, etc., but rather that it is foreclosed to any 'reciprocal' causality exerted through language, thought, or philosophy. Nevertheless, although it has no need of them, it is able to manifest them or bring them forth according to its own particular modality (*if* they present themselves). With philosophy given as a condition, the non-consistency or indifference of the real becomes a transcendental indifference, yet the latter adds nothing to the former.

3.1.7. *Non-sufficiency.* Since the One is nothing but the being-given-without-givenness (of) the One, it in no way produces philosophy or the world (whether through procession, emanation, ontologico-ecstatic manifestation, creation *ex nihilo*, onto-theo-logical perfection)—there is no real genesis of philosophy. This is the *non-sufficiency* of the One as necessary but non-sufficient condition. The real is a 'negative' condition or condition *sine qua non* for...precisely because it is not itself nothingness or negation. Consequently, it is *additionally* necessary that philosophy be given in order for the vision-in-One to be able to give philosophy according to its own mode of being-given.

Philosophy's Effectuation of the Vision-in-One

4.1.1. *The existence of philosophy or the affect of the world, and its real contingency.* The vision-in-One gives philosophy *if* a philosophy presents itself. But philosophy gives itself according to the mode of its own self-positing/givenness/reflection/naming, or according to that of an enlarged self-consciousness or universal cogito. It is, at best, existence and gives itself with the feeling or affect of its own existence ("I know, I feel that I philosophize"), taking the latter to be the real as such rather than merely its own reality. But existence cannot engender knowledge of existence, knowledge that would not be viciously circular. The existence of philosophy amounts to an automatism of repetition that believes itself to be the real because of a well-founded hallucination, a hallucination that only the vision-in-One can expose.

4.1.2. *The effectuation of the vision-in-One by the givenness of philosophy.* Because of its non-sufficiency, the vision-in-One requires that philosophy (which provides a usage of language and of thought) be given in order to be *effectuated.* The effectuation of the vision-in-One does not cancel its status as negative condition, or render it 'sufficient.' Thus, it is neither the actualization of a virtual nor the realization of a possible. It is a sign and witness of philosophy's relative autonomy (one that is not absolute or in-itself) once the latter is given according to the mode of being-given-in-One. It is the taking into account, not of philosophy in general or as supposedly in-itself, but of the autonomy of philosophy, once the latter has been released from the grip of its own hallucinatory absolute form, such that this autonomy indexes philosophy's specific reality and structural consistency as 'philosophical decision.'

4.1.3. *Of non-philosophy as unilateral duality.* Non-philosophy is not a unitary system but a theoretical apparatus endowed with a twofold means of access, or a twofold key, but one that is radically heterogeneous because one of these keys is identity. This is the 'unilateral duality.' Because of its radical immanence, which refuses all positing or consistency for itself, the vision-in-One is never present or positive, it is never given within representation or transcendence, nor is it manipulable in the manner of a 'key.' This duality does not have two sides: the real does not constitute a side, only non-philosophy or philosophy's relative autonomy does so. This is no longer a bifacial or bilateral apparatus like that of philosophy, but rather one that is *unifacial* or *unilateral*. A duality which is an identity but an identity which is not a synthesis: this is the very structure of determination-in-the-last-instance. Non-philosophy thinks without constituting a system, without being unitary. For example, the subject in accordance with which it is produced ('the Stranger') is not something facing me, it is as a uniface and is for this reason a stranger to the world, a stranger to the law of bilaterality which is proper to philosophy and to the world, yet it is not a stranger to the real.

4.1.4. *Contingency and necessity of the non-philosophical effectuation.* Because of the philosophical origin of the material from which its axioms and theorems are drawn, and thus as instance of thought in general, non-philosophy is, from the viewpoint of the One, globally contingent relative to the real which remains foreclosed to it. But as thought determined by the real, it acquires the real necessity of the vision-in-One that is also the transcendental necessity of this real contingency. The One does not legitimate philosophy as it is or as it gives itself, but only insofar as philosophy becomes transformed in its 'being-given.' From the viewpoint of philosophy, non-philosophy is necessary but partly tautological. To think according to the One (to think philosophy according to this mode) is, on account of this aspect, a philosophical objective, one that utilizes philosophical means.

4.1.5. *The being-foreclosed of the real One.* Non-consistency implies or presupposes (these are equivalent here) the being-foreclosed of the real to thought, whether the latter be philosophical or non-philosophical—a thought which, nevertheless, the real is able to give according to its own mode of being-in-One. Consequently, thought does not affect it, the real does not *receive* it but *gives* it and does nothing but give it. That which is given-in-One is without a prior reception. This is its radical autonomy: the primacy of phenomenality over phenomenology, of the phenomenon over the empirico-philosophical model of donation-reception, passivity, etc. The being-foreclosed of the One is not cancelled once there is an explicit effectuation of the vision-in-One by philosophy; it is maintained through this effectuation. This being-foreclosed suspends philosophy's causality with regard to the real, but it does not suspend the entirety of philosophy's causality relative to thought as such, for which philosophy represents a mere effectuating 'occasion.' In any case, this being-foreclosed does not prevent the One from giving (-receiving) thought, language, and, more generally, the world.

4.1.6. *Philosophy's relative autonomy.* Philosophy gives itself as absolute autonomy. The latter is revealed to be the same real hallucination and 'transcendental' illusion concerning the One as was philosophy's sufficiency or pretension with regard to the real. Absolute autonomy is also effectively given—*according to*—the One as a merely relative autonomy. This preserves the autonomy of its reality as occasion and hence as material for non-philosophy. This autonomy is relative insofar as it is limited with regard to philosophy's spontaneous belief, and relative also in a more positive sense insofar as it is now transcendentally legitimated by the real, which ratifies philosophy's structural consistency, its quasi-materiality.

The Cloning of Non-Philosophy on the Basis of Philosophy

5.1.1. Effectuation is the taking into account of philosophy's reality, of its relative autonomy. This reality and autonomy imply that the One no longer gives philosophy just as a mere 'occasion,' but that it fulfils a new role with regard to the latter; a role which is now 'decisive' and which constitutes a positive 'intervention' within philosophy. The real as One thereby assumes a transcendental function, while remaining the inalienable real that it is, without changing in nature or 'becoming' a second, 'transcendental One' alongside the first. This transcendental cloning of the real on the basis of a philosophical material is possible without contradicting the real's radical autonomy since philosophy is already given in-One, and consequently the real does not enter into contradiction with itself by assuming a transcendental role with regard to philosophy. Unlike philosophy, non-philosophy does not proceed from the transcendental to the real (and from the a priori to the transcendental), but from the real to the transcendental (and from the latter to the a priori).

5.1.2. The clone is that which is said of non-philosophy, not of philosophy as material for the latter, and even less of the real which, without being transformed, is rendered agent, *transcendental agent*, of cloning. The non-philosophical clone is in essence or according to its matrix a transcendental instance, which is to say a vision-in-One which is said of this or that material of the philosophical type. It is thus the exact content of all speaking or thinking *according to* the One. The transcendental is a clone because it is said of the inalienable One, but said with regard to the material whose autonomy and reality are now taken into account or introduced. The clone is thus 'transcendental' and not real, but it remains real-in-the-last-instance or, more precisely, the clone is the concentrate of the entire structure of determination-in-the-last-instance as such.

5.1.3. The '*according to*' or clone appears to exceed the One, just as the transcendental appears to exceed the real. In actuality it does not exceed it: it is a mode of the in-One, which does not exceed itself within philosophy by 'becoming' transcendental. It is rather philosophy that exceeds the in-One (duality), but it does not exceed it in exteriority (philosophical dyad) because it is already and in any case given-in-One. It only exceeds the One through its own intrinsic reality 'within' its immanent-being-given or being-given-in-One. Cloning is necessary *if* philosophy presents itself or rather *if* it is taken into account according to its own consistency and autonomy, and it is possible or non-contradictory from the viewpoint of the real.

5.1.4. The clone is not the double of a given identity which is in reality already a double or doublet. It is 'on the contrary' *the real-transcendental but indivisible identity (of) a philosophical double*. The real is not a clone of itself, it is a radically simple identity, neither divided nor even clone (of) itself. But it is thereby able to *determine* non-philosophy (rather than philosophy as such). To clone, to determine-in-the-last-instance, to bring forth non-philosophy: all these formulations express the same operation, and they express it better than would the term 'produce.'

The Subject and World-Thought (Essence, Existence, Adsistance)

6.1.1. Non-philosophy is a globally transcendental discipline, that is to say, a discipline that is real-in-the-last-instance (one that makes use of philosophy's transcendental dimension in order to formulate itself). It is at once the determination-in-the-last-instance of a theory (of a knowledge that remains distinct from its object, adopting a model taken from science), and also of a pragmatics (of a *usage* of philosophy 'with a view to' the non-philosophical subject, adopting a model taken from philosophy). It is theoretical by virtue of one of its models: science. But it is neither a philosophical and therefore self-positing theoreticism, nor a philosophical and therefore self-positing pragmatics. It is theoretico-pragmatic only by virtue of its aspect as a non-philosophical operation, but real or practical by virtue of its cause. Thus, it is not a 'negative' theory-pragmatics either, but rather one requiring that the vision-in-One be effectuated by invariant scientific and philosophical models.

6.1.2. The non-philosophical subject distinguishes itself from the subject of the philosophical type. It is a purely transcendental subject, distinct from the real ego, turned toward the world to which it is a stranger and toward which it turns itself as stranger. But it is ego-in-the-last-instance. The unilateral duality of ego and subject marks the end of their unitary confusion. The subject does not use philosophy as if it were already constituted, it *is* that use. It is not only pragmatic, making use of world-thought, but also and equally theoretical. Moreover, it does not 'do' theory, it *is* the theoretical. *Transcendental science*, which is the *clone* of philosophy-science, is thus the subject as such (of) non-philosophy (the 'force (of) thought'). The subject is theoretical and pragmatic through the scientific and philosophical material in accordance with which it varies, but it is globally transcendental as real-in-the-last-instance, or as ego that clones the real subject transcendentally.

6.1.3. Non-philosophy is the transcendental science that constitutes the essence-of-the-last-instance of the subject—the 'force (of) thought'—one that may additionally be specified on the basis of the particular material indexed by 'ego-subject-other.' Thus, the subject is *existence* solely on account of the philosophy that it integrates, the ecstatic nature of the latter representing its aspect as 'existence.' Accordingly, the complete unilateral duality of the subject cannot be said to 'exist' in general but pertains instead to another structure of thought: it is *adsistance* [*adsistence*], according to a theoretical and pragmatic mode, *of* and *for* world-thought.

6.1.4. Non-philosophy demands the identification of that which is philosophical and fundamental, and that which is regional (art, science, ethics, technology, etc.). But it identifies them only in-the-last-instance, rather than through their immediate confusion or by collapsing one into the other in conformity with the law of their philosophical association or 'mixture.' Non-philosophy postulates the identification-in-the-last-instance, through cloning, of philosophy and world in a 'world-thought.' The hypothesis of a world-thought is one that could be legitimated for philosophical reasons (the 'world' as philosophical concept, philosophy as cosmo-logy, cosmo-politics, onto-cosmo-logy, etc.) and in accordance with the authority of philosophy alone, but this concept partakes of the real contingency of the world in general. Yet it is also amenable to a more profound legitimation through non-philosophy insofar as the latter posits it in a theorem as identity of a clone. It then possesses the 'given' status of an axiom, along with the transcendental status, or status as given-in-the-last-instance, of a theorem 'for' philosophy.

6.1.5. What does this non-philosophical adsistance mean? It cannot 'transform' (produce, engender, create, etc.) the objects of philosophy or the entities of the world. But it can *transform* (cause to occur according to their being-determined-by-the-One-in-the-last-instance, or according to their relative autonomy, or cause to be *brought-forth* through the vision-in-One as cloning) philosophy as a whole which is a self-presenting hybrid of identity and difference. It does not intervene 'within' the specificity of experience, in the manner in which philosophy often and mistakenly claims to, nor does it even provide that specificity with meaning. It is not, generally speaking, an operation or activity to which the subject would remain external. The subject *is* adsistance in its very essence (essence which is without-essence in-the-last-instance). If adsistance is neither interpretation nor practical intervention, it is the bringing-forth of world-thought, one that is practical only in-the-last-instance—the being-brought-forth or being-given which transforms the latter's type of autonomy and liberates it, and thereby liberates the subject (as transcendental identity (of) world-thought), from its entrapment by the hallucinatory belief in its own sufficiency. This transcendental identity, which is that of *philosophy as such* [*la philosophie*], remains incommensurable with 'philosophy' ['*la philosophie*'] in the philosophical sense.

Chapter 2

'I, the Philosopher, Am Lying': A Reply to Deleuze

Translated by Taylor Adkins, Ray Brassier, and Sid Littlefield

Philosophical debate is neither interesting nor perhaps even possible unless it is oriented towards thought's outside: we have to thank Deleuze for having stated this so clearly and in such a rigorously principled manner. However, what is also interesting about this book, *What Is Philosophy?*, is that it espouses philosophical naïveté in a manner that is at once so innocent and so provocative that it cannot but invite us to clarify our ultimate presuppositions with regard to philosophy: this book pushes us into a corner and forces us to put our cards on the table. Not only is it difficult to sustain this refusal of *disputatio* without fail for anyone who also recognizes in it the essence of philosophy's agonistic style, its 'guerilla warfare' (if not its 'war for laughs'); moreover, it is also necessary to explain the abandonment of dispute and its justification in the

This essay was written as a response to Deleuze and Guattari's 1991 book *Qu'est-ce que la philosophie?*, which appeared in English translation in 1994 as *What is Philosophy?*, tr. Hugh Tomlinson and Graham Burchell (New York: Columbia University Press, 1994). Laruelle's "Reply" was first published in French in *La non-philosophie des contemporains*, eds. Laruelle et le Collectif (Paris: Kimé, 1995). An English translation of Laruelle's text, from which the present version is modified, appeared in *Pli: The Warwick Journal of Philosophy* 20 (2009).

essence of thought and the real. The ultimate residue of any critique of communication is to communicate one's reasons for abandoning communication. By simply mocking the excesses of the 'communicational' ethos, as Deleuze and Guattari do, one risks appearing genuinely naïve in espousing the rights of philosophical naïveté or philosophical faith. Philosophy has never been a 'Sermon on the Mount' promising the 'Beatitudes of thought' to idiots. It would at least be wise to recall that the philosopher who passes for the paragon of dogmatism is also the one who inscribes communication and the epistolary 'relation' into the essence of being. But perhaps the example of Leibniz shows that his concept and practice of communication are themselves dogmatic and destroy or reify themselves, as witnessed by his own philosophy's overall failure to communicate itself? Is this very paradox, now inverted, not the one that affects Deleuze's philosophy, much communicated but little understood, and still less utilized?

This problem is undoubtedly undecidable in philosophical terms, given that each philosophy has its own concept of 'communication,' and thereby scrambles the coordinates or codes which might allow one to obtain an 'objective' evaluation of communicational and non-communicational powers, and of the power of miscommunication, whose combination defines the philosophical. On the other hand, a book as largely successful and as assured of its own power as *What Is Philosophy?* does such a good job of transmitting the affect of the philosophical at the expense of science and even of art—not science 'itself' or art 'itself,' in practice, but rather the philosophical concept of science or art, not cinema 'itself' or in practice, but rather the concept of cinema—that the pure revolt of 'science itself' and of 'art itself' as immanent concept-less practices, legislating for themselves independently of philosophical authority, cannot but rise up against such a self-assured philosophy. 'It is right to rebel against philosophers': here it is philosophy in its greatest triumph that incites rebellion. Perhaps it is precisely at the point when the philosopher seems to acknowledge the autonomy of science and of art that he most subtly denies it. For it is precisely the book's 'concordant' or at least 'vicinal' style of reciprocal respect—which it undoubtedly opposes to communication—which is most dangerous; its most inapparent ruse, but also the remedy itself for anyone who knows how to see in this its ultimate trick. That philosophy's self-affirmation or re-affirmation is directed against its historical and worldly precariousness can embarrass only other philosophers. On the other hand, the eroded pedestals which are set up for science and art once more oblige thought to posit the hypothesis that an 'art-thought' and a 'science-thought' are possible and must be attempted, given that they cannot be re-affirmed in the manner in which philosophy is.

So how are we to turn this book into a problem—but a problem of a new type, since it is already itself the solution to the problem of what a problem is? Let us suppose that there exists a book called 'What is philosophy?' and that it claims to answer this question by virtue of its own existence or manifestation. Thus it is impossible to talk about it: because this book is at the center of philosophy and philosophy is at the center of this book; because *philosophia sive natura* and one does not converse with God; because one does not communicate with natural phenomena; because one does not argue with Spinoza. This is an absolute book: it writes and speaks itself, it makes itself and responds to the question: "What can a book do? Specifically, what can a book of 'philosophy' do?" with the answer: it can only write itself. And what can the readers of this book do, other than get off on a philosophy that unfolds without them?

All that remains then is the tone of familiar and vesperal conversation between friends, a conversation about the Elder and the Stranger, and the non-philosopher come to tell the marvelous story of philosophy—this is also the tone of this book, its 'unbearable lightness,' midway between the philosopher's confession of faith and the fairy tale in which he in his dotage takes delight. We cannot give in to it further. Because if it is a question of doing what the authors have done rather than of saying what they have said, perhaps there still remains one last situation they have not foreseen: that of really doing what they said they did or what they have only done by saying, mixing doing and saying once more under the name of 'creation,' as all philosophers have. It remains to do or to practice, solely to practice, the immanence that they say and which is perhaps still only that of philosophical saying: it remains to practice immanence with regard to their saying-of-immanence. Not to comment on this book, or turn it into a problem, is perhaps no longer to want to do anything besides what they have done. Because to try to deconstruct *What Is Philosophy?*, to oppose to it once more Wittgenstein, Heidegger, or Derrida, would be at once too easy and pointless or impossible: How can one deconstruct the very event of philosophy, Christ and Spinoza-Christ? On the other hand, perhaps it is still possible to really do what they have thought to do—the real here perhaps no longer being the other of philosophy?

I. The Imitation of Spinoza and the Gospel of Philosophy

The book is a curious dialogue among the living dead, a theater of dead figures who still live through the becomings or metamorphoses that convey them—a muffled dialogue. There are the Greeks—Socrates and Plato rather than Epicurus or Lucretius. There are Spinoza, Nietzsche, Bergson—the fetish-triad: Benedict, Friedrich, Henri and the others, or the facts of philosophy. There are Kant and Husserl—the bad side of philosophy, its derivative aspect, its ghetto—yes: they are 'ghetto' philosophers. And further along there are the great 'communicationalists' of contemporary philosophy. Then there is Christ as function of singularity or empty-square of the event, of the once-and-for-all, occupied by Spinoza, a Spinoza more Christlike than Christian, for whom Christ is a new mask—a place perhaps also occupied by Dionysus, whom we should not forget, since between Spinoza and Nietzsche Christ has finally been crucified or re-crucified. The philosopher's confession of faith consists entirely in this imitation of Spinoza, the prophet of immanence: whoever has seen Spinoza has seen philosophy in all its glory. Philosophical faith is no longer an awaiting, but its self-realization is not its suppression: on the contrary, its *parousia* is its existence as such, which here means its becoming: a complete or natural faith. Spinoza realizes philosophy just as Christ realizes faith: we will say in both cases, according to two possible formulations, that they both realize a faith-for-all/once-and-for-all [*foi(s)-pour-toutes*]. This is a philosophy-for-all, if you will, which is another way of saying the One-All.

How can we hide it? Are we not rather surprised by this return of the 'grand style' in philosophy and this rivalry with Plato, Spinoza or Hegel? The philosophical scene, scattered, communicational and planetary, is all at once surveyed by a *philosophia* that is very close to being *perennis*; eternal at least through its fixed survey or co-extensiveness, a co-intention to itself or its becomings. Our authors still believe in logic, not of the Anglo-Saxon variety of course, but in logicity such as it is represented by the Spinozist attribute, the Nietzschean perspective, or perhaps by Hegelian logicity. In their own way, they ceaselessly polish the great mirror, that of Wittgenstein, or of the thousand surfaces of the plane of immanence, which they fold and refold precisely in order to prevent it from shattering, from being disseminated or plunged into another immanence, that of language games or textual forces, for example. They ceaselessly repeat that it is concepts that 'show themselves' and do nothing but show themselves. They continually call for the definitive silencing of logic, a formula that is not simply negative. They do not like history, which is probably too 'uneven' a terrain for them. And they prefer to smooth out becomings that, in order to be recounted by one whom they themselves call an idiot, are perhaps lacking, for some of us at least, in the sound and the fury that typify modernity. The event is Stoic, but it has a tendency to Platonize in a frenetic manner; and the private man who accompanies and endures these becomings remains in the eye of the storm, there where a peace reigns that is no doubt strange, but a peace nonetheless.

It is as though this overly eternal book misses both philosophical modernity and the Judaic turn that has determined a large part of philosophy in the twentieth century. In Hegel's judgment, for example, Deleuze would also lack the 'principle of personality' concomitant with reflection and the Kantian discovery of subjectivity. Nevertheless, the book is constantly evoking Hegel or aligning itself in some way with him: through the concept as philosophical activity; through Christ as emblematic figure of the event of 'philosophy,' of its completion and opening; through the circle of auto-position; and through the positivity of the infinite. Yet it is impossible to speak of a 'return to Hegel.'

As for the Judaic turn, the book retains of it the mere minimum that is tolerable for philosophical authority; the homeopathic or Spinozist dose, rather than the Levinasian or heteropathic dose. It is obviously the infinite which is in play here, and the Other, or Others, the Friend and the Brother, who are placed at the opening of the book are there as a signal and a declaration: we Spinozists are also contemporary! Let us consider these two points and test on them this mitigation of Judaism, this sort of cruel mildness of becomings through which Deleuze resolves every conflict.

With regard to the Other, far from being the infinite beyond the concept and beyond the world that holds me hostage, it remains a concept and a world—a 'possible world' no doubt, but a world nonetheless. Moreover, here is a Nietzschean philosopher who has friends rather than disciples, and whose principal affect may well be fraternity, but as becoming or passing through: we are not brothers, we become them, which is another way of refusing to be the keeper or hostage of the Other man. Nietzsche saw Spinoza as his 'big brother.' We will not say that Deleuze is the little brother of these two, but that he is the other brother—rather than being otherwise-than-a-brother. This affect of fraternity is not sufficient to establish a democracy, nor does it found one here, without it being a question of a disguised return to an essentially aristocratic community. What interests Deleuze is what happens or passes between democracy and aristocracy. The essence of philosophy accomplished as becoming is therefore certainly not 'democracy'—not, it seems to us, in any sense of that word; not just in the sense of liberal democracy or the ethics of the Other human being.

As for the infinite: if Deleuze, like all philosophers, has only ever had one problem, it is indeed this one. It is no longer a question of thinking the infinite ("How can 'I' as a finite being think the infinite?"), but of 'infinite' thinking. All that is required for this is to allow the infinite to think itself. Because the infinite itself is thought out, a triad is necessary: initially, an auto-position or an auto-production, later that of desiring machines, and today that of concepts; next, a plane, the full body without organs, and today the plane of immanence in the state of fixed survey; finally, a consequence follows, an inevitable marginalization of the human subject as action and passion; one could say 'man enjoys' [*l'homme jouit*] with the same reservation with which Spinoza said: 'man thinks.' This, however, is the machine designed to resolve the problem of the infinite. Yet there still remains for it to produce something. For what is the philosophical discovery proper to Deleuze, given that his is not a philosophy of objects or theses, but of machines, and given that his work does not possess the thematic unity of a treatise and cannot be decomposed in the traditional terms of objects, themes or methods, since it is composed solely of functions? His specific philosophical discovery is not the Spinoza-Nietzsche-Bergson triad, since he is not a historian of philosophy, contrary to what some maintain, but rather the fact that he sets philosophy in-becoming. This is not the event, for the Stoics had already discovered it, nor the multiple, which can be attributed to Nietzsche. Perhaps it is the infinite power of the event; the power of infinite variation proper to Spinoza, Nietzsche, and Bergson; in other words, philosophy at the point at which it is fulfilled and flows through itself like the chimerical water-fish. Deleuze's specific discovery is infinite, unlimited becoming as principle of solution and variation in thought, or principle of 'creation.'

Since we have evoked Christ and the good news, we will say that Deleuze is philosophy's John the Baptist; but an *a* posteriori John, who is obviously opposed to Paul, and whose task is to open our eyes to the unique event which forces thinking, but which, being unique, can only be repeated or raised to the power of the infinite. Whence Deleuze's practice, which consists in potentiating philosophers, turning them into events, becomings, *jouissances*; in continually changing concepts without ever changing operations; in masking Spinoza, Nietzsche, and others. Whence Deleuze's ethos: man is at home not 'in' the infinite, but as the infinite's neighbor—an infinite becoming-ethological, if you will. Whence Deleuze's ethics: the imitation of Spinoza-Christ; the always partial identification with philosophers; wisdom as creation, but as eternal creation, a gentle or weakened creation, since nothing is created *ex nihilo*. What Deleuze, fusing Nietzsche and Bergson, calls 'creation' is this infinite operation or *causa sui*; this commentary—now eternal—focused on history; an almost divine commentary which, instead of extracting meaning from history hermeneutically, extracts operations from it, draws out events from it, makes proper names surge forth. Deleuze has rediscovered a secret—the secret or what is proper to philosophy, a secret that he would have us believe is very old and was once lost. He rediscovers the philosophical idiom, which has however become foreign to itself, but which remains an idiom precisely insofar as it has become the language of the infinite. The language of the good news is at once absolutely private and absolutely universal. Their coincidence marks the apex of the philosophical community's self-contemplation. Whence Deleuze's ostentatious horror at consensus and communication, which are transcendent artifacts.

II. Response to Deleuze's Objections about the One, Science, and Non-Philosophy

Deleuze sets out three objections—whether explicitly or implicitly—to what we call 'non-philosophy' and opposes another concept to it, precisely a concept of non-philosophy:

1. The One which non-philosophy thinks would seem to be a 'One-All close to Spinoza'; the implication being: it is merely close, not exactly identical, and this for the following reason:

2. It effectively gives rise to a science, rather than to (as it should) a philosophy; 'non-philosophy' should also be a non-science.
3. Lastly, an objection that is implicit but that can be inferred from the text: 'non-philosophy' claims to be external to philosophy, the science of the latter, whereas it ought to be a presupposition that is internal to philosophy.

It is striking that these three objections, mutually implicating, are founded upon a fundamental misunderstanding, a hasty and theoretically deficient interpretation of the One, which is the central problematic of non-philosophy. We will respond to each of these three points.

1. First objection:

The One that is at issue here, the radical immanence in terms of which we define it, is above all *not* the One-All, whether 'close' to Spinoza or not, but rather a One-without-All, or even a One-without-Being, which we call the One-of-the-last-instance, the better to contrast it to the convertibility, which it refuses, of the One with Being, as well as to the Spinozist reversibility of the One with the All. Certain contemporary philosophers abhor the One—and with good reason. So do we: the proviso being that this is the One that is correlative—no matter how and regardless of the relation—to the Multiple, just as it is convertible, whether via an inversion or not, with Being. Whether the One prevails over Being or the Multiple, or whether the Multiple prevails over the One, or whether alternatively they prevail over each other: these are all clearly possible solutions that must be investigated—but this is precisely not our concern. A real critique of Deleuze's conception of immanence is now possible, and among other possibilities, it can be carried out in the name of a form of immanence that is more radical still, one that expels all transcendence outside itself: not only that of theological objects and entities, but also the ultimate form of transcendence, which is that of auto-position or survey, of the fold or the doublet, etc. The One-of-the-last-instance is the true suspension of this One-All and, more generally, of all reciprocity, which is to say, of every possible relation without exception, even that which is allegedly 'without relation' to Being.

This rules out the following two metaphysical interpretations of what we call the thought of the One, or non-philosophy: (1) the One as One-for-All, the Once-and-for-All of the event. This is ruled out since the One essentially has no need of the All and is not alienated in it, even if the All requires the One. (2) Conversely, the One as All-for-One. This is also ruled out because that which is not the One, i.e. being as multiple or as science, is relatively autonomous, specific, and forms an instance that is irreducible to the One, in which it nevertheless has its cause, but a cause which is only of-the-last-instance. This type of causality reciprocally guarantees to the One-real and to (transcendental) science their respective autonomy. 'Science' is by the One, not for the One.

2. Second objection:

The One-of-the-last-instance gives rise to or causes a thought which cannot be science rather than philosophy, but is rather the unified theory of science and philosophy, which must consequently be understood as a 'transcendental science.' For us as well, science is solely by virtue of its essence the authentic 'ontology,' except that it is no longer a philosophical logos. Accordingly, being here is no longer auto-position: this is the sense in which it is inconsistent or non-consistent—it is no longer the Being of philosophical ontology. It is deposed by the One, absolutely de-auto-positioned by it, which also ensures its character as multiple, and hence as a philosophically inconsistent multiple. Ours is no longer the traditional conception of science in terms of a philosophical triad posited a priori (concepts, plane of immanence, conceptual personae), of which science would still be in spite of all a degraded form, in a state of decline or deceleration relative to the chaos of infinite speeds which philosophy alone preserves (triad of the function, the plane of reference, and partial observers). Science as 'unified theory' is rather the first and only thought issuing from the real as One-of-the-last-instance, and that has as its object the inconsistent multiple, which it inhabits, and whence it can, under certain conditions, be elaborated as science of the One itself.

3. Third objection:

Non-philosophy is not a presupposition that is internal to philosophy, the plane of immanence other than the concept, both internal and external to it; rather, it is what philosophy becomes under the conditions of its unified theory with science. It is not internal and external to philosophy, but comes after it as the result of the work this discipline carries out on its philosophical material. Thus it is not simply the other of philosophy, or a new version of the Other, since far from still being internal to philosophy, it is radically heteronomous relative to it because it has its cause in the One rather than in the Other.

'Non-philosophy' has an ambiguous valence: it is a new commodity that circulates on the philosophical market only at the risk of the gravest misunderstanding. We have never understood this term in the same sense as Deleuze-Guattari, who seem well and truly intent on using it to recuperate non-philosophy for the benefit of philosophy's authority. On the one hand, non-philosophy as we understand it is not intended to introduce into philosophy a form of alterity that is still masterable by the latter and deployed, as we see in this book, in order to exalt philosophy's hubris and authority unreservedly, despite all the precautions taken to render adjacent, and merely adjacent, philosophy, science and art. For on the contrary, such adjacency does not destroy the ancient hierarchical and aristocratic ideal characteristic of all philosophy. From the outset, non-philosophical practice is instead intended to revoke philosophy's authority without destroying philosophy, which is still required as the datum or phenomenon of a new science.

Moreover, if our idea of non-philosophy does not correspond to the problem of rendering the philosophical idiom foreign to itself while simultaneously preserving it, this is because it is the solution to an entirely different problem: that of determining a more theoretically rigorous form of thought, one that is simultaneously more universal and 'real' than philosophy, and that converts the latter into a particular case, or perhaps, a simple 'model' of thought.

It is not a question of introducing science into philosophy under the conditions of the latter, while taking its validity for granted, or of turning philosophy into a science, as Husserl, following many others, sought to do. To put it in terms whose schematic nature we are well aware of, it is a question of transforming philosophy into a simple variable, and of treating the One-real and the aprioristic structures of science as constant functions or relations, in order to deduce non-philosophical statements from them.

Lastly, these rectifications also amount to a real critique; not so much of Deleuze-the-philosopher as of the philosopher in Deleuze, as well as of the philosophy that proceeds by way of this type of falsification, which always expresses a resistance.

III. Tableau of Principal Distinctions

We will call 'restricted' non-philosophy the type that still has its site in philosophy, which remains the master of its alterity or limitation, and 'generalized' non-philosophy the kind that issues from the vision-in-One and is effectuated as the unified theory of science and philosophy, generalizing philosophy under non-philosophical conditions. We will use the following theses to contrast these two types on a certain number of points:

1.1. In restricted non-philosophy, which issues from Spinoza and Nietzsche, the One and the Multiple, Being and the One, the One and the All, are reciprocally predicable, no doubt according to that radical form of reversibility which destroys their metaphysical forms but reaffirms or intensifies the great axiom of their convertibility, which is foundational for philosophy.

1.2. In generalized non-philosophy, the One and the Multiple, Being and the One, the One and the All, are no longer reciprocally predicable. And this irreversibility is absolute: it is not subject to a reversal of their hierarchy or to an inhibition of their reciprocity. There is a new disposition of the One, of Being and beings, through which they are henceforth measured by the causal relation that we call 'determination-in-the-last-instance,' in which the One precedes Being without any sort of alienation.

2.1. The immanence of the One-All remains that of a plane or a universal over-determined by the multiple; it is an 'immanence to self' where the 'to' indicates an ultimate intentionality and hence a positionality. It is an auto-positional immanence that remains restricted as immanence because it wants to encompass Being or the universal, because it perpetuates at its core the form of transcendence itself, if not transcendent entities, and because in doing so it inhibits itself.

2.2. The immanence of the One-without-All is no longer auto-positional but precisely non-self-positional or non-self-thetic; absolutely devoid of the very form of transcendence, which constitutes the fold, survey, and becoming. Insofar as immanence constitutes a break, it passes between the One and the All, rather than between the One-All and its modes, which are said to be, in a very limited and restrictive way, 'transcendent.'

3.1. The multiple according to philosophy remains imprisoned by the One-All or consistency under the aegis of the 'auto-' or of over-position [*sur-position*]. This kind of multiple is not originarily delivered from consistency; consequently, its inconsistency necessarily appears, despite all precautions to the contrary, as a lack of determination or as insufficiently determined.

3.2. The multiple according to non-philosophy is transcendentally constituted by the One-of-the-last-instance; admittedly, starting from the philosophical multiple or from the mixture that is the One-Multiple. But, on the one hand, the One suspends the consistency that the latter achieves through auto- or over-position, and, on the other hand, it determines it as a radically immanent multiple. Being is neither a plane nor an ecstatic horizontal project; neither an infinite plane nor a full body whose horizon would become a line of flight.

4.1. The non-philosophy that follows from Nietzsche and Spinoza constitutes a limited and still philosophical attempt at the solicitation of philosophical authority; one moreover whose potency [*puissance*] relative to that of deconstruction could be debated, and if not 'decided,' then at least measured by the comparative force of the affects or the real of which each is tributary.

4.2. The non-philosophy that follows from the vision-in-One, rather than from a philosophical decision, and that is effectuated as a radically inconsistent multiple (in other words, 'opposed' not only to the scientific but also to every philosophical form of consistency, and to the particular hierarchy of Being, for example), begins by globally suspending philosophy's authority, without however destroying or denying the latter, but rather delivering it over as a mere material to the operations of a 'force (of) thought' which is only the concrete form of this determination-in-the-last-instance.

5.1. Restricted non-philosophy is restricted by restricting the reality of science in relation to philosophy, and conversely, by ultimately allowing philosophy to posit itself as primary and as guardian of the real, which here means the One-All. The infinite potentiation of metaphysics—as 'superphysics'—even more than the deconstruction of metaphysics, begins by postulating philosophy's authority over the real, and consequently by devalorizing science, even if it marks a certain progress by making science a kind of other neighboring philosophy.

5.2. Generalized non-philosophy starts from a basis of thought which is itself neither scientific nor philosophical—the One as cause-of-the-last-instance (the 'force (of) thought'), rather than as philosophical presupposition; but it shows how this One is only thinkable through a thought that utilizes philosophy as its material or phenomena, rather than through a philosophy, whose authority is suspended from the outset.

6.1. Restricted non-philosophy is merely a presupposition of philosophy, a dimension of the latter rather than its essence or its becoming. It is a condition of philosophy that the latter must overcome, and one that remains under its authority.

6.2. For us, non-philosophy is an absolutely specific program of thought—and one that is absolutely positive, rather than just a heteronomous relation to philosophy. It entails more than just the refusal of philosophy's authority: an alternative use of philosophy, but one that is positive as material for, and particular case (or model) of, non-philosophy. Non-philosophy is a program that is carried out immanently.

IV. The Problem of Immanence: The Case of Spinoza

If there is one problem that traverses contemporary philosophical research, it is, more even than the multiple, the problem of immanence. The approach to the One is split between two poles: (1) The One as All, obtained by reducing the grossest forms of transcendence, rather than transcendence as such: this is the solution that runs from Spinoza to Deleuze. (2) The One as auto-affection or immanent 'radical' life, which retains the general form of the cogitative ego, and which is compromised by a treatment of transcendence that is itself transcendent. Even if 'life' is the method, there persists an ultimate atmospheric transcendence, an ultimate empiricism in the critique of the latter: this is Michel Henry's solution.

Against both solutions, yet in closer proximity to the second, we propose the One-of-the-last-instance as immanence devoid of ontico-ontological content; immanence which is therefore no longer thought as following from an act of givenness or auto-affection, which is to say, as a function of transcendence, in opposition to which this immanence would be characterized as ego.

With the problem of immanence, we find ourselves treading a thin line where everything can either be lost or saved. It is a question of knowing whether immanence will be the real as immanent only (to) itself; or whether it ultimately remains the property of a plane, a universal, or even an ego.

For how in fact are we to ensure a priority for immanence without neglecting or denying transcendence? Where do we draw the line of demarcation, and is it in fact a question of drawing a line? Furthermore, does immanence necessarily form an infinite plane, an infinite speed, if, in fact, it does not necessarily form a space of reference defined by axes or coordinates? Rather than starting from the One, Being, the Other, or beings, Deleuze starts out with these two operators that separate them and that are like the pairs of coordinates with which he constructs both nature and thought. But precisely, he draws a line of demarcation, he dismembers this pair and selects immanence 'alone' as the element of thought, globally rejecting transcendence as theology, illusion, and servitude. Such exclusive selection is characteristic of philosophy; a selection which in fact surreptitiously reintroduces the other term and resorts to it unknowingly, thereby reconstituting a coupling, a reversibility more profound than any explicit thematization of reversibility.

Why, for example, the 'in-between-two,' the 'in-between-time,' the 'in-between-multiple,' 'eternal becoming,' etc.? Because of a mixture deeper than any survey, auto-position or plane of immanence, and one that explains each of these: the mixture of immanence and the multiple, i.e. transcendence. Yet the problem of immanence remains completely original and specific. Deleuze collapses it too quickly onto that of the multiple, without giving it its due; the multiple being his initial problem, the one to which immanence is subordinated. But the relations of the One and Being are specific and original, and are irreducible to those of Being and the Multiple, of Being as One or as Multiple. Moreover, it is pointless to claim to have clarified the status of Being and the proper content of transcendence so long as immanence of itself has not demonstrated its non-convertibility with transcendence.

Between immanence and multiplicity, i.e. transcendence, things stand as they do with every contrasted couple: philosophy starts out from their more or less reversible pairing, such that neither term is adequately and definitively elaborated, with both circulating together, back-to-back, in the indefinite circle of reciprocal determination. By way of contrast, a non-philosophy that is a unified theory requires that immanence be initially given and ensured, even if only to guarantee the reality, rigor, and non-circularity of its reasoning. Only then, from this secure foundation, will non-philosophy begin to elucidate the essence of the multiple that fills out the (non-)real, the void of Being, and its mode of being-given after the One and in accordance with the data of philosophy. Non-philosophy identifies each order in its absolute or relative autonomy, without conflating them or pushing them to a state of fusion or indiscernibility.

The injunction 'immanent to itself rather than to something else' is in fact imperative, yet it conceals an indetermination, an ultimate ambiguity. An amphiboly is harbored by the 'to' of 'to itself,' one that reintroduces not 'things,' i.e. reified transcendences, but the pure form of transcendence itself as distance or relation, as surface or universal plane. Obviously none of this is characteristic of traditional metaphysical or dialectical thought: it is not the scission of an identity, or the indivisible and coextensive distance of unity. The philosophically normal but theoretically amphibological concept of 'plane of immanence' means that immanence continues to orbit around the plane and as plane; it continues to orbit around the 'to' ('to itself') as axis of transcendence. Immanence thereby remains 'objective,' albeit devoid of any object; it remains the appearance of objectivity, and gives rise to a new image of the real and thought. Instead of being absolutely faceless and unenvisageable, it assumes the face of a plane, of a topology, of survey and contemplation. The Spinozist philosopher draws the line of demarcation between a Being that is devoid of beings, but always in a state of auto-position, and beings as 'transcendent' entities—between a field of presence and present objects—instead of drawing it primarily between the One and Being, or between the real and objectivity.

Has transcendence then really been abandoned? The transcendence of transcendent things, or ontic transcendence, undoubtedly has, i.e. the object-objectivity doublet, but no more. First there still persists a residue of the object, an ontic residue: beings appear here as a system of flows and partial objects, or as the indiscernibility of concepts via 'bridges' and 'zones'—this is what remains of the old 'object' of idealism when it has passed through the millstone of the Mœbius strip. What then remains of Being is the plane of immanence or the full body without organs, the strip itself, which is precisely transcendence's immanent internal form, but never a real immanence. Immanence is no longer 'to' the other in the sense of an ontic object; but far from being radically 'to' itself, it is still 'to' pure transcendence, 'to' the pure form of transcendence. We see why in this type of philosophy—but the problem is invariant—only pure transcendence can finally be said to be immanent to itself, and why behind the given there operates the giving-machine or the plane of immanence that has to reappear behind 'concepts.'

In non-philosophy, there is no longer a 'line of demarcation' that is able to pass between Being and the One, and as a result, the philosopher's favorite operation is deposed. The 'to' of the 'to itself' is undoubtedly foreign to self-consciousness and the intentional subject. But this is too easy a victory. It conceals one final form of transcendence and even of intentionality: the superior form of a distance of the topological kind. And this all the more so given that a genealogy of its transcendent forms (in phenomenology, for example) is possible, starting from the plane of immanence. If concepts correspond to substances with attributes, or better still, to Nietzschean hierarchies of forces, the plane of immanence is the unity of these substances; a unity possessing at least the same general structure of coupling, giving it an infinite power. Whence the concepts of fusion, penetration, indiscernibility, and consistency, which are undoubtedly opposed to the transcending of existence, but by globally incorporating the All or the essence of transcendence into immanence, via a new type of sublation that is non-dialectical or non-Hegelian. Whence this geology or stratigraphy, which masks the Nietzschean spirit of hierarchy: the fixed survey of the concept or plane; the auto-position of the concept as surface or absolute volume; the stratigraphic stacking of the layers of the plane—all forms which presuppose the fold.

One could also speak of over-position rather than auto-position, yet this would change nothing in the principle of the solution. What is called immanence is in reality also position and transcendence: their pairing is the passage or becoming of the in-between-two; not a synthetic unity that is ontological and 'transcendent,' but a unity through the becoming of this in-between-two. The plane is a continuous passage to itself, and hence survey or over-position. There is no transcendence in immanence, at least not in Husserl's sense, but there is their co-intention, that which passes or happens between the one and the other.

The upshot is that the One is always Other and identity always marginal; yet inversely, thought is always at the heart of the Other. Immanence loses its form as subject, ego, or consciousness, just as transcendence loses its form as *meta* and becomes super-ascendance. No more terms, nothing but becomings: the solution is guaranteed not by movement as such but by its infinite power: speed as infinite or indivisible.

Spinoza, thinker of immanence? This is a historical simplification. In reality, Spinoza has always been invoked for two contradictory reasons: for the immanence characteristic of causality, no doubt, but also for the transcendence that is just as characteristic of the unity of substance relative to the so-called 'human subject,' the supposed bearer or site of immanence. We retain the expression 'human subject' here, but it is obviously ambiguous (which subject? which human?). This double enlistment is significant: Spinoza is indeed immanence in effect, but immanence insofar as it is lived or received as transcendent by the human subject, not only external to him or her but also—let us note this formulation—too great for him or her; something Deleuze himself acknowledges and avows, rejecting man as the third and final moment of the triad, as a part adjacent to machines, or as a persona adjacent to concepts. Consequently, there is no essence or absolutely autonomous form of man here: the latter is a system of effects and is composed on the basis of what he contains: affections and perceptions.

The argument given is the following: immanence is not 'to' something else, which is always transcendent; so it is not 'to' the cogito or the ego; it is 'to itself' but not 'to him or herself' (emphasized on p. 208, so that the following is implied: the ego is merely a preliminary form, transcendent to the immanence of the One-All). What is this argument worth? It begs the question: if immanence is that of Spinozist substance, then it is indeed the ego that is now a transcendent form; but this is already to assume what must be demonstrated. Recent interpretations of the cogito (by Michel Henry and Jean-Luc Marion) are more subtle and reveal radical immanence, without representation, to be its essence. The ego can then be defined by radical immanence, rather than the other way around. The problem is crucial. No doubt, whatever the solution, if man is re-submerged into pure immanence, then one turns him into what Deleuze calls an idiot. But since there are (at best) two kinds of immanence or real, there will be two idiocies. If immanence is absolutely devoid of transcendence, the ego or man will be a transcendental idiot. If, on the contrary, as in Spinoza and Deleuze, it includes the pure form of transcendence, then man will be at once a transcendental and a transcendent idiot, which is to say, half-idiot and half-philosopher—a concept which, from our point of view, is rather transcendent. What does this mean?

That man will be split and barred by the unity of substance: there will always be man in general or nondescript man, and the philosopher. Of course, this will no longer be a duality but a subject-in-becoming, an unlimited becoming-idiot or becoming-philosopher, since these are obviously the same. In other words, we find here once again, under the mitigated form of an unlimited becoming, the distinction between man and philosopher, their hierarchy in spite of all: the philosopher who constructs the system and the idiot whom he talks about and who doubtless stumbles through the windings of the system do not adequately coincide. Once again the philosopher does not really want idiocy, he limits it. One has to admire Deleuze's softening of philosophy's old barbaric manners (those of metaphysics, insofar as it was born on the Eastern edges of Greece): he civilizes philosophy, even granting it the faculty of taste. But the problem of what philosophy is, what its existence means, and what its values are worth, is nonetheless left unresolved despite this new gentleness. And Spinoza is only the Christ of immanence, just as Deleuze is only its evangelist. These two have stopped believing in God and Grammar, but they still believe in Christ and Philosophy.

V. The Multiple: Consistency and Inconsistency

As for the multiple, it is posited as primary—as Being itself is—and hence encysted in the consistency of auto-position, of the in-between-two or of hierarchy. As in Bergson, there are apparently two types of multiplicity that form the extremities of becoming. But the residual dualism that kept them separate in Bergson is gone here: true multiplicities are becoming, that which passes from one type (to) the other. The philosopher cannot be indicted of monism or dualism. Nevertheless, or perhaps because of this, he consummates philosophy's unitary style, and it is this very adroitness that arouses suspicion. By way of contrast, non-philosophy would have distinguished two genuinely heterogeneous types of multiplicity, rather than their becoming-identical, becoming as in-between-two or the in-between-multiplicities as the superior unitary form of all multiplicity. Non-philosophy distinguishes on the one hand a philosophical multiplicity which may be of one or several types—the difference is irrelevant here because these multiplicities realize the same invariant through their variations: the invariant that demands that multiplicities be either variations (philosophy), or variables (science), or varieties (art). And on the other hand, non-philosophy distinguishes a type of multiplicity that is absolutely inconsistent or non-consistent, in the sense that it is no longer 'set-theoretical' or calculable, but also devoid of every form of auto-position. Only a 'non-Cantorian' multiple is capable of filling the void of Being as element of thought. This non-Cantorian concept of the multiple, in its 'unilateral' duality with the mathematico-philosophical multiple (and its numerous varieties), is deduced from the One's determination-in-the-last-instance of Being as void, as irreality or (non-)reality. The essence of thought harbors not only an absolute inconsistency, a suspension of arithmetico-philosophical consistency, but also the radical intrinsic consistency or 'finitude' of the One itself—this is a property of thought that cannot be inferred inductively from any existing science. The liberation of the multiple, its relative autonomy, must be achieved with regard to the philosophical gesture of auto-position, rather than with regard to the real. The science of philosophy subordinates the multiple to the One-real, rather than turning it into a new idealist absolute through auto-position.

VI. Deleuze's Topo-Logic: A Transcendental Mœbius

The fundamental unity proper to the marvelous machine that operates 'to' infinity is the unity-of-survey, the unity-of-sliding, the plane that propagates itself up to and including the point of torsion in which front and back are identified. Every philosophy gravitates around an imaginary model of the relations between thought and the real, a dynamic schema of the Same as both of these at once. In this instance, this infinitely disguised, universal paradigm is the Mœbius strip. What was for Lacan merely one topology among others, and what Derrida claims to have shattered and disseminated (the 'double-bind'), Deleuze massively invests in materials that are indefinitely possible and in any case contingent.

The strip, the immanent plane, is the co-extension of front and back—their auto- or over-position. The latter is also equivalent to any of its points, the 'concepts' that participate in the same general auto-position. Over-position is this coincidence-of-becomings, this identity in the form of the becoming of the 'two' sides of the strip. And the strip is what passes from one side to the other, the indivision of a very rapid inversion; the in-between-sides or in-between-laterality, the continuous passage beneath which their identity is given.

Let us consider the points on the surface. They are 2 and 1. Each is two or 'divided,' but the 2 is immediately 1, 1 as becoming however, not as transcendent unity. On a Mœbius strip, it suffices to fix a point for the latter to assume the form of a desiring machine or a concept: the identity of this point, of the front/back, is that of a becoming-one, of a force that is spread out across the strip and unlimited, but with a force that is already double, of two forces in opposite directions.

Any contrasted pair or dyad is thereby spread out in the manner of a strip that is at once infinite or completely straight, and fastened to each of its points. The famous Nietzschean problem, which is not that of opposites but of the passage from one opposite to the other, finds its solution in the Mœbius loop and its eternal or infinite return. The identity of opposites loses its transcendent form as 'Being' and assumes the form of 'becoming' or of the 'strip.' If Being is never definitively lost and must 'recur,' it will recur as the very return of becoming, its objective appearance, its co-extension to-itself or its survey.

In a sense, neither the 1 nor the 2 are metaphysically primary: they are always co-present. Nevertheless, in philosophy's triadic system, their necessary combination (the mixture or dyad) is variable or proceeds via inversion. What is primary is the 2, becoming, 'force' or 'concept,' doubtless in a state of auto-position or 1, but forming the first multiple, which is 'working' and 'productive.' The 1 itself recurs or returns as second, as plane of immanence, but this 1 of the plane is immediately two for itself and in its own manner. For the 1 and the 2 can be treated in turn as the front and back of a 'strip.' It is inevitable that they be identical (this is becoming) up to and including their inversion (this is the plane). Whatever diagram organizes the philosophical decision, the latter is decision and starts with the 2, with the multiple, with intuitive diversity or experience, etc., and transcends towards the One, even if it sometimes does so also as One. The 1 loses its classical transcendence as third term and merges with the 2, which is now becoming. However—this is the 1's rage to exist in philosophy, which is to say, in spite of it—it is not immanent to the becoming of the 2 without also being exterior or supplementary to it, without recurring as 1 that assuredly contains the 2 in turn (the plane of immanence is over-flight [*sur-vol*], level with itself, over-position—a distance now flattened in the One, while remaining a pure distance). There is no third term for a synthesis, but there is a triad, an alternative organization of the subject (3rd), the object (1st), and their correlation (2nd).

Every philosophical pair is subjected to this logic: for example, nothing can be done with a single type of multiplicity, two are necessary—yet this does not amount to a metaphysical dualism since genuine multiplicity is becoming or in-between-multiplicity; that which passes from one to the other and which is primary in relation to one and the other. This is the fundamental basis of Deleuzian logic: the becoming constituted by the multiple is itself multiple: undivided partial force, the concept as bridge or zone, the passage which is not and which will be or will find its being beyond itself by dint of not being. As for the third element of the triad (action and passion, affection and perception), it suffices to pass from the 2-that-becomes-1 to the 1-that-becomes-2 for this passage to be the intersection but also the trumping of the first element of the triad by the second.

If there are points on the double surface, there is also the single strip that accompanies each of its points. Granted, there is no longer a subject behind the act, no subject or object, no Being or big One behind the 2: the big One has become the little 1 that is the fold of the 2. Yet there is still the All and the One, the system of desiring machines or concepts, and the plane of immanence that accompanies them. There is still the shadow or outline of the All to survey the concepts or objects/flows. There is still a presupposition to condition the production of concepts; a secondary but persistent presupposition, which is never abolished. It is true that there is no longer a 'metaphysical' world-beyond, but there remains the pure form of the world-beyond as plane of immanence, the full body or system that falls back upon its machines or concepts. Desiring machines or concepts are absolute machines or 'absolute volumes'—they are not drawn from a larger machine, they are not abstracted or extracted from a greater volume. But this single volume or machine from which we think we have finally been delivered, necessarily recurs as what must be able to accompany the parts or pieces.

The man inside the philosopher cannot stop rubbing his eyes in the face of these revolutionary marvels to which philosophy claims to accustom him and through which it distracts him. Instead of the overtly classical hierarchy of Whole and Parts, philosophy's new conjuring trick inverts the relation: the parts come first (absolutized as 'partial objects,' etc.), then comes the All—an All that is without parts, but that prowls at the horizon, in the vicinity of the parts. This is an All that has become smooth and ungraspable, and hence all the more monstrous—an All to be feared. The philosopher begins as a great Greek infant and ends up as a little postmodern child.

VII. What Is Thinking? A Scientific Problem

These problems intersect with another whose solution dismembers the venerable Parmenidean matrix: Being and thought are the same. The philosophical gesture is woven from idealism: through it, the given is not simply reduced to the real ('Being'); it also includes thinking, which is also essentially supposed as given, but in forms that are transcendent rather than deduced from the One-real alone. Thinking becomes a problem, as opposed to an all-purpose solution, when it ceases to be traced from some instance of knowledge or perception, or extracted from experience, and is introduced into the question: How can we still think when the One alone is given? How can we still think Being and thought when there is nothing but the One-real which is given without any presupposition? Between the given (the One) and the data (philosophy), it is the philosophical type of presupposition, Being and the plane of immanence, that must be excluded on behalf of a presupposition without auto-position, in order to deduce the essence of thought from these two types of cause. Philosophers never begin without taking too much for granted; without 'presupposing,' which is to say, auto-positing beyond the given. They already know what thinking and Being are—they assume the validity of philosophy itself—whereas non-philosophy knows only the given and discovers the form of thought that sets them 'functionally' in relation. Philosophers assume philosophy in order to prolong it, reaffirm it, or even deconstruct it, but what they fail to grasp is that they, the hunters of presuppositions, continue to be fascinated by the phantasmatic belief in presupposition. Let us call 'non-philosophy' the manner of thinking that does not know a priori what it is to think or to think the One. It no longer possesses an idea of science, or an idea of the idea. Its only project is to think the One, and consequently, all it has, alongside the One, are the data of philosophy, now available as material. Philosophers have known from all eternity the idiom-of-the-real, for they assume that it has one; but non-philosophy 'knows' only the real, possesses only it or is possessed by it alone, and makes of the discovery of this idiom and of its usage according to the One a testable theoretical hypothesis; a problem that can no longer be resolved by philosophy, but whose solution requires the latter. The One is the first and not the last cause of thought; or rather it is the last-instance cause of thought; a thought that is not the result of a method or operation. Thought becomes a problem whose solution is deduced from the One as absolute given.

VIII. Axioms of a Non-Spinozist Thought

Let us imagine a Spinozism that is a transcendental science rather than the exaltation of philosophical naïveté—hence, a non-Spinozism. Here are some of its axioms:

1. The One is in-One—it desubstantializes itself—rather than the One-of-substance or reversible with the latter.
2. What divides the One from substance, or even the One (of substance) from its attributes, is a unilateral distinction rather than a line of demarcation.
3. The One is cause-in-the-last-instance (of substance or) of the attributes rather than simply expressing its essence in the attributes.
4. The 'attributes' (Being and thought) reflect or express the One in their transcendental essence, without the One expressing itself in them.
5. The 'attributes' are determined-in-the-last-instance by the One and occasionally by the data of philosophy.
6. Given the One-in-One or One-of-the-last-instance, and given the data of philosophy as 'modes,' what ensues for the 'attributes,' that is, for Being and thinking?

Instead of trying to understand (as Althusser tried to) the causality known as 'determination-in-the-last-instance' in terms of the Spinozist model of immanent causation, but an immanence that is still impregnated with transcendence, it is time to change hypothesis, to invert the order of explanation, and to flatten Spinoza out along the axis of determination-in-the-last-instance conceived as causality of the most radical of immanences; to treat Spinozism (and Nietzsche, and Bergson…) as mere philosophical data, as 'modes' of the One and of the Being that follows from it. We thereby arrive at a usage of Spinoza that is occasional rather than imitative; and at a 'knowledge of,' rather than an 'identification with,' Spinoza; at an occasionalism for him and for all philosophies.

What would it entail to stop imitating Spinoza? Not changing behavior, selecting one ethos while abandoning another, but changing our experience and our knowledge of behavior, as well as of philosophical ethics as the superior form of behavior, thereby conducting philosophy's etho-logos towards a non-ethology or a non-ethics. That thought could be conceived as an 'ethology,' albeit of the 'superior' or 'transcendental' type, can only inspire disgust: man is neither plant nor animal, whether terrestrial or celestial, nor even a becoming-plant or a becoming-animal—yet it is still necessary to feel (*sentir*) this rather than to resent (*ressentir*) it and let it be lost in resentment and repression. Against infinite variation, against Spinoza's infinite variance or potentiation, let us pit a non-Spinozism that is more universal still; one for which Spinoza himself will be no more than a model or a restricted interpretation. It is a matter of stripping-bare the Spinoza-event, rather than of making it flash forth in Heraclitean fashion, and of returning it to the multiplicity and the chaos which inhabit the void of thought.

IX. The Last Philosophical Antinomy: 'I, The Philosopher, Am Lying'

What is philosophy's relation in man with what is given in 'experience'—whether real or illusory, it matters little—with history, the sciences, and the arts? That of allusion. Allusion, this ludic touching that culminates in pleasure, is the relation internally determined by the Mœbius strip, by its topological properties and its data, whether 'metrical' or otherwise. Immanence here serves to save transcendence by detaching it from its empirical conditions as well as from transcendent entities. This is the superlative realization of the secret ambition proper to all philosophy: to use the One to rescue Being or the All, to use immanence to safeguard Being from the prestige of beings. The One ensures philosophy's allusive character, since Being, as infinite, can be no more than a simple allusion to beings, given that it is no longer intrinsically affected and conditioned by the latter, as it is in 'metaphysical' representation or even in Heidegger, by virtue of the finite reception of beings. Transcendence is in any case already an allusion to…beings, but philosophy is the systematic form of this allusion. What is called 'becoming,' for example, is an allusion to history, which it does not touch without also overcoming-surveying. What is called 'philosophy' is an allusion to culture, science, and art, and 'the One-All close to Spinoza' is an 'allusion' to the One-of-the-last-instance…An allusion that feeds on these only in order to slip among them for an instant and then escape them.

The consequences for 'empirical data' are disastrous: not only are they deprived of reality, they are also, above all, necessarily conceived as deficient or degraded, as the reification or 'actualization' of becoming. Their reality is an illusion, an appearance, a deficiency of their auto-position in and by the strip. That which is 'auto-'posited (just as one says 'suicided') and posited by what is more powerful than it, by the Mœbian form of all auto-position, is not posited in itself or by itself and must sever all continuity with its 'double' or empirical 'indication,' or construe it as mere appearance. This is the most general presupposition of every absolute idealism, and perhaps of all philosophy, an idealism that is here equally an absolute realism ('real without being actual, ideal without being abstract')[1]: 'experience' is generally construed from the outset as devoid of reality. Because of their reversibility with philosophy as the understanding of problems, evil and stupidity are

1. *What is Philosophy?*, p. 22. –Tr.

appearances without consistency or reality. Indeed, there is no absolute evil, only a reversible or mutable stupidity. Experience is suicided by philosophy, even and above all when the latter is an absolute empiricism; experience and many other things besides: man, suicided by philosophy…A system of flight, and of flight as self-enjoyment. A superior politics of desertion, an abandon that is 'superior' because it harbors its own rationale. Never has a work of philosophy exhibited with more impudence and perhaps even probity—or naïveté—the philosophical lie while deriving such a powerful enjoyment from it.

Like any great work that has attained its own perfection and manifested its own force, *What Is Philosophy?* pushes us towards an exclusive alternative; one that is exclusive beyond even the philosophical inclusion of alternatives, in a disjunction where philosophy is merely a solution alongside another that is 'entirely' other, rather than the entirety of solutions. But this is an alternative that destroys itself as such, as disjunction in general, constraining us to renounce the false dilemma—either philosophy or science—in the name of a constraint more vibrant than fulgurating: given the One, what ensues for the One-All? What ensues for philosophy? Non-philosophy is this result.

We are now ready to formulate the final problem.

If this book proclaims, more naïvely than ever before, philosophy's idealist lie, and if it is philosophical par excellence (this is its naïveté), is it truly capable of telling this lie or is it lying once more? Does this double lie constitute a new truth or simply a new abyss for truth? Let us give the paradox of Epimetheus a slightly more interesting form by generalizing it: "I, the philosopher, am lying" as the paradox of all possible paradoxes. In order to dissolve this antinomy, which is more powerful than others, would not a radical, absolutely transcendental concept of science be necessary, rather than a weak and 'logical' concept of thought as science? Not a philosophy or a logic of science, but a veritable transcendental science—not of science—but of the essence (of) science?

X. Philosophical Survival and Life Itself

We would like to be able to say: none of this is against Deleuze—such a perfect philosopher—but all of it is 'against' philosophy. Yet it is impossible to make this distinction: the major risk taken by Deleuze—against everything most critical and most tormented in modernity, though this is not our problem—is precisely that of having identified himself unreservedly and without remainder with philosophy itself [*LA philosophie*], with philosophy playing with itself—immersing himself within it in an uncritical identification. Deleuze not only refuses to take seriously the latest outrage committed against philosophy, the latest assassination attempt—the Judaic one, which pits Levinas against Spinoza—he also conflates his own identification with the pure transcendence of philosophizing—his own immersion in transcendence transcending itself—with the immanence for which he would like his operation to pass. Nothing of philosophy or of philosophical understanding is foreign to him—he has invested in it with an alacrity that is disconcerting—and yet he seems not to have heard the news so unsensational that no philosophical 'communication,' nor even the critique of non-philosophical communication, has managed to transmit it to him, which is the fact that philosophy can only claim to be consummated in joy or *jouissance*, rather than perishing of nihilist inanition, as is the case for its adversaries, because it is stillborn, born-as-dead, a mere allusion to life…Let us risk saying it in Deleuzian style: it is an after-life [*sur-vie*]…Those who confuse philosophy's factual death with that of God, Being or the Subject should stop making us laugh. But he who has confused philosophical passion with life will hardly have made us laugh any less. Philosophy's avidity for 'life' and 'joy' inclines towards the grave. It is a premature birth kept alive only through artificial means; an abortion that draws life from those who identify themselves with it. It needs this identification to survive. But we who provide it with life, will we one day be capable of no longer lying in the name of survival and of recognizing what is in fact the case: that we continually judge survival in the name of life?

Chapter 3

Controversy over the Possibility of a Science of Philosophy

Jacques Derrida and François Laruelle
Translated by Ray Brassier and Robin Mackay

JD: Mine is not an easy task. After what you've just heard, you can see the risk I took in speaking of François Laruelle's '*polemos*.'

You spoke in the name of a certain peace. Yet I have to admit that, with regard to *polemos* and terror, there were moments while I was listening to your description of philosophical terror as transcendentally constitutive of philosophy, etc., when I was sometimes tempted to see in your own description a rigorous analysis of what you were in fact doing here. I say sometimes, because I did not succumb to the temptation. I shall nevertheless attempt to say something else. I am obliged here to play devil's advocate.

This debate followed a conference on "The Community of Researchers," held under the auspices of the Forum of the College Internationale de Philosophie, Paris, in 1988. Jacques Derrida had agreed to open the discussion. A transcript of the debate, "Controverse sur la possibilité d'une science de la philosophie," was published in *La Décision Philosophique* 5 (1988), 63–76. The English translation of the discussion appeared on the ONPhi website (www.ONPhi.net) in February, 2005.

Among the many questions I would have liked to ask you, slowly, patiently, text in hand, in the manner befitting a philosophical society or a scientific community; from among all these questions, it seems natural for me to pick a few and to formulate them in a schematic fashion, since we don't have much time, and to refrain, at least for the time being, from referring to your latest book[1].

I shall state in a word or two, bluntly, the questions which occurred to me while listening to you, and my perplexities.

Would you say that the scientific community, the community of science, of the new science which you described, is a community without a *socius*, in the sense in which you defined the *socius*?

This question is not about whether or not you have been cautious enough, but rather about the way in which your precautions run riot and counteract one another. When you talk about the essence of science, while being careful to say that what is at stake is this essence prior to its political and social appropriations, which is to say prior to what is called its effectivity, its effectivity rather than its reality—where do you find this essence of science, which science in its effectivity always falls short of? What is it apart from its effectivity, its political and social appropriations? This is a very general question, which I shall naturally try to reiterate by means of other questions which I have prepared.

My first question—a big one—concerns the reality of this real which you constantly invoked in your talk, or—and this comes to the same thing—the scientificity of this science, this

1. *Les philosophies de la différence. Introduction critique* (Paris: PUF, 1986). Published in English translation as *Philosophies of Difference: A Critical Introduction to Non-Philosophy*, tr. Rocco Gangle (London and New York: Continuum, 2011). –Tr.

new science, since this reality and this scientificity seem to be related. You oppose reality to a number of things; you oppose it to totality—it is not the whole, beings as a whole—and you also stressed its distinction from effectivity and possibility. The distinction between reality and possibility doesn't look all that surprising. But what is rather more surprising is when you oppose reality to philosophy. If we were to ask you in a classical manner, or in what you call the ontologico-Heideggerian manner, "What is the reality of this real?," and whether it is a specification of Being, you would I suppose dismiss this type of question, which still belongs to the regime of ontologico-philosophical discourse, and even to its deconstruction, since it is easy to assimilate the latter to the former. Such a question would still be governed by this law of philosophical society to which you oppose this real, the new science, community.

What makes it difficult to go along with the movement I would like to accompany you in, is that it sometimes seems to me to consist in you carrying out a kind of violent shuffling of the cards in a game whose rules are known to you alone... Which is to say that the hand ends up being completely re-shuffled. The only thing is that I seem to detect—and this is probably a philosophical illusion on my part, one which I would like you to disabuse me of—a real and philosophical program which has already been tried and tested. For example, when you say:

> By way of contrast, one can ask another question, one about [science's] conditions of reality. I am careful not to say 'conditions of possibility,' these being the State-metaphysical interpretation of science combined with the philosophical-metaphysical interpretation, whereas I am talking about science's transcendental conditions of reality...

Under what conditions is research a real activity as opposed to a social illusion? This is all the more crucial given that you go on to state:

> The problem then becomes that of a critique of reason [let us say heuristical]; of a real rather than merely philosophical critique.

Is this distinction pertinent for a transcendental philosophy? Can a transcendental philosophy distinguish between the possible and the real in the way in which you yourself do?

I should say that I often felt myself in agreement with you. For instance, with your initial description of the researcher, of research insofar as it seemed to follow a certain Heideggerian logic, in the description you gave of the principle of reason, and what you said about programming and about non goal-oriented research, which in fact reinstitutes a goal.... I was willing to subscribe to all this. Then you went on to oppose to this description this new science, which you distinguished from its political, social, etc., appropriations, and there, obviously, I had the impression you were reintroducing philosophemes—the transcendental being only one of them—into this description, this conception of the new science, the One, the real, etc. There, all of a sudden, I said to myself: he's trying to pull the trick of the transcendental on us again, the trick of auto-foundation, auto-legitimation, at the very moment when he claims to be making a radical break. So if, for example, the distinction 'real/possible' is pertinent independently of philosophies of the transcendental type, another hypothesis arises, which I immediately have to dismiss along with you: isn't this distinction already characteristic of a Marxist or neo-Marxist type program? Real and no longer philosophical: at least insofar as the philosophical would seem to be restricted to a theoretical rather than transformative interpretation and hence would remain confined to what you call the social illusion. But you rule out this hypothesis for us by telling us that when you say 'real,' you are not referring to material structures. So I seemed to understand that this kind of Marxist-style interpretation was also among the things you wanted to rule out.

You claim that:

> This amphiboly of philosophy and the real, which is the secret of philosophical decision, can only be discovered in accordance with another, generally non-philosophical experience of the real.

Here, I would like you to explain very pedagogically what you mean by a "generally non-philosophical experience of the real."

You also claim that:

> Philosophy and unconstrained research are the abundant forgetting of their real essence; not of their conditions of possibility but of their conditions of reality. There is no forgetting of philosophy; on the other hand, there is a forgetting by philosophy as principle of sufficient philosophy of its own real essence.

A little further down, we encounter this notion of 'force,' about which I have many questions I would like to ask you:

> [I]t is this latter thesis that must be radically contested in order to found a critique that would be more forceful than all the deconstructions of philosophical sufficiency.

This motif of force reoccurs forcefully but associated with a project of auto-foundation, of transcendental legitimation—

these are the terms you use, albeit in inverted commas, and my question concerns these inverted commas. I could have been very quick and simply asked you: What is the status of inverted commas in your text?

For example, when you say, "This instance must be real rather than material; it must be of a cognitive order in order to measure up to philosophy and to research; finally, it must have its foundation and legitimation in itself, without requiring the mediation of philosophy, which is to say it must be transcendental in its own way"—my question, my perplexity, the point on which I am asking for illumination is: What is a transcendental project of auto-foundation and auto-legitimation when it is non-philosophical? And when you then go on to attribute this non-philosophical project of transcendental auto-foundation, auto-legitimation, to a science, to what you call science insofar as you distinguish it from all of its appropriations, and which you also call the force-of-thought (you yourself underline the definite article), my question is: What is it in this force, this science, that is not philosophical, etc.?

This force will be a force capable of—I don't want to go too far and say that it will be capable of imposing peace—but it is nevertheless a force in the name of which the peace proper to this community founded by the new science will be possible. What is this force belonging to a subject whose undivided identity, without identification, anterior to division, will ultimately found a community? When one knows, having read you, that the One to which you refer in your discourse, and on the basis of which you critique—you prefer 'critique' to 'deconstruct'—or rather send philosophy packing; when this force, this subject, this science, this undivided subject, is a 'One' which you tell us is not the identical, must not be understood in the classically philosophical sense of 'One'; what then is the difference between this One and the entire chain that accompanies it, i.e. science, the real, the entire community, enforced peace, free peace?

What is the difference between this One and what others call 'difference,' since it is not identity?

Ultimately, all the questions I wanted to ask you come down to this schema: Why do you reduce—and isn't there a violence here of the kind you denounce in philosophical society?—so many gestures which could accompany you along the path you wish to pursue? To take just one example among many: the gesture of proposing scientific approaches which would no longer conform to the conception of current practices, to the philosophical concept of science; of interrogating certain discourses which claim to be scientific; of helping science make critical progress through movements which would no longer conform to what is understood in those appropriations which you talked about.

Why ignore the existence of this gesture in the various deconstructions which you evoked in passing?

Why, in this or that approach putting forward propositions very similar to your own—for example, with regard to constitution, given that you said that some things were unconstituted—why class these gestures among everything else you dismiss? It is obvious that among movements of the deconstructive type, which you have thought about and whose analysis you have developed at greater length in your book, there is among other things a movement to deconstruct the model of constitution, to avoid that constitutive or constitutional schema which you identify with everything you want to reject.

Why proceed thus, if not on account of a gesture tantamount to socio-philosophical war? There, bluntly put, are all the questions I would like to have been able to formulate better, in a situation other than one of improvisation and haste.

To what do you tie your concept of democracy? What does 'democracy' mean, once this concept is emptied of all its philosophemes?

FL: I notice that all your questions are interrelated, obviously; they form a coherent whole, just as one might expect. These questions are indicative of the resistance of the principle of sufficient philosophy.

JD: No surprise there, needless to say…

FL: Which is to say that your questions have a very particular style, which I found highly interesting, that of retortion: "You're just like those you criticize"; "You're doing just what you claim to abhor." You taught me in your work that one should be wary of retortion. So I would like to suggest that to the extent that you are making a certain use of retortion, and this is a theme that recurred throughout, right up to the end via the accusation of socio-philosophical war, then it is necessarily the case that some of your objections in a certain way maintain precisely the opposite of what I said.

Let me take your first question. You tell me I am practising terror [*prostestations from Jacques Derrida*].

Do I practice terror? There are obviously two readings of my text. There is a philosophical reading, one in which I do practice terror. And there is a non-philosophical reading, which is obviously my reading. And from the latter point of view, I am reluctant to concede that I am practising terror. I would like to suggest to you why not.

I was careful to say that terror was bound up with overturning. I only used the word 'terror' in contexts that related it to overturning.

So, are the relations I described between science and philosophy relations of overturning?

Absolutely not. The whole problem for me, having studied your work along with that of other contemporary philosophers, lay in defining a point of view on philosophy that would not be acquired philosophically; which is to say, a point of view that would not be acquired via philosophical operations, be they those of doubt, controversy, or overturning as principal philosophical operation, and even displacement insofar as it is of a piece with overturning. From science to philosophy—and I will return to this point, since this is the direction that governs everything I write—there is no overturning. There is merely a limitation, but one which does not take the form of an overturning. Perhaps it should be stated more explicitly: there is a limitation of philosophy by science; that is all. But I absolutely do not overturn philosophy; were I claiming to overthrow it, it would be a pointless gesture, a zero-sum game. The entire enterprise would then be contradictory.

JD: When you say you are calling into question the sufficiency of philosophy, in what way is that particular gesture different from a host of others, mine among them…? Why erase the latter gesture and consign it to the realm of sufficiency?

FL: You often claim that I conjoin ontology and deconstruction. Obviously, I only conjoin them under certain conditions, not generally, and I have sufficiently emphasized in other works how seriously I take the difference between certain forms of metaphysics and your own work on and in metaphysics. But if I allow myself to conjoin them, it is in the name of the struggle against the principle of sufficient philosophy, and in that regard alone. What is more, I do not call any philosophy into question, since I posit the equivalence of all philosophical decisions.

What is probably wounding for philosophers is the fact that, from the point of view I have adopted, I am obliged to posit that there is no principle of choice between a classical type of ontology and the deconstruction of that ontology. There is no reason to choose one rather than the other. This is a problem I discussed at great length in my book[2]: whether there can be a principle of choice between philosophies. Ultimately, it is the problem of philosophical decision. And I sought a point of view—one may then query the way in which I arrived at it, or constituted it—which implies the equivalence of all philosophical decisions, or in other words, what I call democracy and peace.

Obviously, I defined democracy and peace only insofar as these might be pertinent for a community of philosophers, and only within the bounds of that framework. So I am in no way conflating your work with a classical ontology, not at all. But in the name of the principle of sufficient philosophy, given that I adopt a point of view which allows one to uncover this principle, I am obliged to stipulate this equivalence, because the principle of sufficient philosophy cannot be discovered from within philosophy; it can only be discovered from elsewhere.

But I would like to return to this point about terror, because it is really close to my heart.

There is no overturning of philosophy. There isn't even a reduction in the Husserlian sense, or a bracketing of philosophical decision. There is, if one wants to take up the term reduction—but you will take me up on my use of philosophical vocabulary so I will come back to this in a moment—what

2. Ibid. -Tr.

I call an already accomplished, already actualized reduction of philosophical decision by science. Because science is precisely not constituted in the way in which a philosophy is constituted, through a set of operations among which there may be transcendental reductions; science is already a transcendental reduction in act. And that is why the order I follow, the real order, is the order which proceeds from science to philosophy. If you follow the opposite trajectory—and as a philosopher, someone who is in a certain sense governed by the principle of sufficient philosophy, you cannot but follow the opposite trajectory—you will necessarily register my gesture as a particularly aggressive one. But I am bound to tell you—and this is the consistency proper to my own position—that your impression of terrorism and aggression is an impression that is internal to philosophical resistance; it is a mechanism of philosophical self-defence.

On then to the second problem, that of the new science. It seems to me that, unless I made a mistake, I did not speak of a 'new science'?

JD: I am absolutely certain you did.

FL: If I did then it was in a certain sense precisely a philosophical lapse. Philosophy is always stronger than one imagines. In no way do I want to talk of a 'new' science, precisely because what I mean by science is what everyone else means by science. What I don't want to do is reiterate the philosophical distinction between the so-called empirical sciences and transcendental science. This is precisely the distinction I don't want to make because to do so would be to reconstitute a hierarchy whereby philosophy can characterize itself as thinking while relegating science to the status of a merely blind, technical production of various kinds of knowledge.

Since my concept of the transcendental differs from the use to which philosophy puts it, likewise, my concept of the empirical will also differ from its use in philosophy. For me, all the sciences, even those philosophy degrades by calling them 'empirical'; all these sciences partake of transcendental structures. They are already consistent in themselves, they already have access to the real. On the other hand, what is possible is a science, maybe a new one—or at least one that could be called 'new' insofar as it still has to be constructed—a science that I will call transcendental and whose goal will consist simply in describing the transcendental constitution of those sciences which philosophy calls 'empirical.' But this transcendental science is not superior to those empirical sciences, since it no longer relates to them in the ways in which philosophy related to them. It is a science that is absolutely on the same level as the others. There is in a certain sense a community, a kind of equivalence among all sciences, whether ordinary or transcendental. I wanted to break the relation of domination which philosophy enjoys over the other sciences.

JD: This is what you wrote:

> Thus a community of researchers in philosophy will be democratic and peaceful only if it refrains from founding itself upon the principle of sufficient philosophy in order to consider itself as the subject of science. And if it then contents itself with treating philosophy simply as the object of a new science and new practices elaborated upon that foundation...

FL: What I describe with the term 'essence of science' are the structures of any science whatsoever. Once these transcendental structures have been elaborated, or rather once these already existing structures have been described (it is not my description which creates them), it then becomes possible to envisage a specific science *for* philosophy and to extend, so to speak, scientificity as I understand it to the study of philosophy itself. So in this sense, yes, there would indeed be a new science to create, but the science I describe is the most banal, most ordinary kind of science.

You also asked me: Isn't there also a *socius* in science? Yes, obviously; I alluded to it when I said, with regard to the politics of science, that the latter are an overdetermination of transcendental structures, which I have not analyzed here. I left it to one side precisely because it is an overdetermination. But obviously, the sociological, political, economic intrications of science need to be analyzed, and its transcendental structures include or may be affected by the effective conditions for the production of forms of knowledge. I do not deny this.

You ask: Where does this essence of science come from?

This is obviously the principal question, in a sense, because it means: From where do you derive what you are telling us? There are two ways of answering this question: a philosophical answer, which I don't want to give, and a rigorously transcendental answer. The philosophical answer would be to say: Having reflected upon the philosophical decision and the ultimate prerequisites for transcendence, for the mixture of transcendence and immanence, I concluded that philosophy assumed something like the One, that the One had always been presupposed by philosophy, but that the essence of the latter had never been elucidated by philosophy.

But I have to say that this answer did not satisfy me at all, because it led me to position myself in your territory, which is that of philosophy, and to want to give a 'false' (the term is not quite right) description of what is at stake. The true answer I must give to you—maybe it will seem rather cavalier to you—but ultimately it is just as simple as the question:

"Where do I get this from?"

I get it from the thing itself. This is as rigorous an answer as I am able to give. Because the criterion for my discourse is a rigorously immanent or transcendental criterion, there is no other answer I can give on pain of placing myself upon the terrain of effectivity, and I neither can nor want to think science on the basis of transcendental effectivity.

JD: I don't understand what 'transcendental' means outside of philosophy. But when you tell us: "My answer is the thing itself," I want to put two questions to you: Isn't this a philosophical move, the appeal to the thing itself? What; which; *what is* the *thing itself*?

FL: The One is the thing itself.

JD: You think that the relation to the One as the thing itself is a non-philosophical relation or experience?

FL: Yes, precisely because it is not a relation. This is the crux of the misunderstanding, which is to say that you insist on wanting to make a philosophical reading, through the prism or optic of the philosophical decision, albeit a decision which has been worked upon—you persist in trying to read what I am doing through the medium of philosophy.

No doubt, you will object: "But you yourself constantly use philosophy. In the name of what do you allow yourself to use the term 'transcendental' or the term 'One' if not in the name of philosophy?"

I have to tell you that this is an absolutely standard, normal, common objection; it is always the one people put to me first: "You use philosophy in order to talk about something which you claim is not philosophical." Listen…the objection is so fundamental that it is tantamount to indicting me of a crude, rudimentary self-contradiction. It is entirely obvious that I allow myself the right, the legitimate right, to use philosophical vocabulary non-philosophically.

It is a defining characteristic of philosophy, of the principle of sufficient philosophy and its unitary will, to believe that all use of language is always ultimately philosophical, whether sooner or later. Philosophy, which I characterize as a 'unitary' mode of thought, cannot imagine for an instant that language can be used in two ways: there is the use of language in science, which is not at all philosophical, contrary to what philosophy itself postulates in order to establish itself as epistemology or fundamental ontology of science; and the use of language in philosophy. Philosophy postulates that every use of language is a use with a view to the logos, or what I call a use-of-the-logos, language being taken as constitutive of the Being of things. From this point of view, if this were the only possible use of language, then obviously an escape from philosophy would be out of the question. But I postulate—actually, I don't postulate it, since I begin by taking them as indissociably given together from the outset—the block of the real as One and a certain use of language which corresponds to this particular conception of the real. Since I take as indissociably given from the outset a certain use of language, which is not that of the logos, and the One which founds it, I do not contradict myself, I do not relapse into philosophical contradiction. Philosophy has a deeply ingrained fetishism, which is obviously that of metaphysics, but which may not be entirely destroyed by philosophical critiques of metaphysics, and this is the belief that ultimately all use of language is carried out with a view to Being, in order to grant Being, or to open Being, etc.; that all use of language is 'positional.'

But science—I don't have time to develop this here—makes a non-positional, non-thetic use of language. There is an entire theory of scientific representation waiting to be elaborated, because the latter does not have the same 'ontological' structure as philosophical representation. I think that most of the objections put to me are a consequence of this belief that there is only one use of language, and that not only does Being speak through language, but as soon as you begin to speak, it is ultimately Being that speaks and you are no more than an intermediary. It is this belief that science extirpates. That is why I allow myself the right to use the term 'transcendental' under conditions that are no longer ontological, my only problem then being to display a requisite degree of internal rigor or consistency, which is to say, to transform the word 'transcendental' so as to render it better suited to describe this non-thetic experience which the One is. So if I continually oppose the One of science, which from my point of view explains scientific thought's profoundly realist character, its blind aspect, its deafness to the logos, its unbearable character for philosophy; if I distinguish this particular One from philosophical unity, this is for reasons that are relatively precise, ones which provided the starting point for these investigations. It seems to me that philosophy cannot help but deploy itself through a hybrid structure that combines transcendence and immanence. Whatever their modes, however varied these two coordinates, philosophical space is a space with two coordinates, transcendence and immanence. It may be that metaphysical transcendence has a kind of tain or lining of alterity; that may well be possible, in which case there would no longer be just two dimensions, but three or four; one could try to discover them. But it seems to me to be a defining characteristic of philosophy to combine something like a position with something like a decision, and hence to deploy unity, but to always deploy unity along with its opposite. This opposite may not always be immediately given, one may have the impression that it has been expelled from immanent unity, but in reality transcendence returns in the form of a pedagogy: you are told that the soul has to identify itself with the One…Philosophy thereby shifts to a pedagogical stance which reintroduces transcendence, and as a result the One of philosophy…(there is no doubt that the subject is obliged to identify with the One) simultaneously transcends the subject.

But I claim that science's paradoxical nature for philosophy, its fundamentally obscure, non-reflexive character from the viewpoint of philosophy—which explains why philosophy has denigrated it throughout the centuries, since Plato at least and right through to Heidegger ("science does not think")—follows from the fact that with science immanence is given right from the outset in itself and solely by itself. Absolutely immanent data, Husserl used to say, are devoid of "the slightest fragment of worldliness." I am in fact very close to Husserl, obviously, but with one slight difference, which is precisely the crucial, non-philosophical difference, and which is that with Husserl, in spite of everything, a transcendental reduction is required in order to actualize the transcendental ego. But I claim that in science, no preliminary transcendental reduction is required: we already necessarily start from the One. Which obviously seems very odd: this is not where we expected to find science! We start from the One, we don't arrive at it. We start from the One, which is to say that if we go anywhere, it will be toward the world, toward Being. And I frequently use a formulation which is obviously shocking for philosophers, particularly those of a Platonist or Plotinian bent: it's not the One that is beyond Being; it's Being that is beyond the One. It's Being that is the other of the One.

Hence this great upheaval, this seismic shift in philosophical concepts, which philosophy is in a certain sense obliged to suppress. But as I have often repeated, it is neither a permutation nor an overturning.

As for the distinction between the possible and the real, obviously, it is initially a philosophical distinction. But in philosophy one distinguishes between the empirical real and the possible (the a priori), and then the real of possibility; one envisages a synthesis or mixture of possibility and the real. All I am saying is that science is a type of thinking that is realist in-the-last-instance and that it is exclusively realist. At least initially, or in-the-last-instance, because obviously I have not developed the analysis of science, particularly the problem of objectivity, which would have complicated matters a bit. But science in its principle or absolute foundation does not acknowledge the possible, it knows only the real. Obviously, it will make use of the possible and effectivity, but it will make use of them on this basis, which is to say that contrary to philosophy, which very often starts from the empirical in order to posit the possible or the a priori in opposition to the empirical—and you know all the problems this generated for Kantianism, and how the neo-Kantians tried to overcome this problem of the a priori posited in opposition to the empirical, a problem the disciples of Kant and Fichte were already aware of—science starts directly from the One, which is to say from the most radical experience there is. You have to start from the real, otherwise you'll never get to it.

Who *wants* the real? Philosophy. And because it wants the real, it never gets it, which is to say it has *realization* instead, in other words, war.

You asked about the force in whose name peace is imposed.

If I grant myself this force as One, through a use of language which corresponds to this anteriority of the real over representation, then I am quite straightforwardly obliged to deduce peace from it, an undivided peace, as I said; I must deduce it from science, I cannot do otherwise, it is simply a matter of rigor. So either you're saying that this entire project is an act of force, in which case, obviously, all of its details are also acts of force; or we have to start from this One and this real.

As for this interpretation in terms of an 'act of force,' I am perfectly willing to acknowledge its plausibility if I position myself on the terrain of philosophy. But I think that once one has, not made the leap, because it is precisely not a leap, but rather realized the 'stance' proper to science, there is no act of force. I did not claim to be exiting philosophy, that is not my project at all… My project is quasi-scientific and science is not governed by any practical ends, at least not to my knowledge. In this regard, I am very Spinozist: all teleology must be absolutely eliminated. Science contents itself with description and my attitude is purely descriptive. In reality, science contents itself with describing the order of the real, and the order of the real goes from science toward philosophy. It is philosophy which transcends science; science is not some sort of black block or black transcendence for philosophy, contrary to what some claim.

I understand why one may have the impression of terrorism or of a totally uncompromising set of demands. I believe that in theory there can be no compromise, unless compromise is constitutive of the real. But since I don't believe that compromise is constitutive of the real, I make none; I content myself with being consistent, which is to say that I try to develop a rigorous science.

Chapter 4

Translated from the Philosophical: Philosophical Translatability and the Problem of a Universal Language

Translated by Ray Brassier

Of Philosophy as a Universal Language-Thought or Principle of Sufficient Language

By what right does one raise the problem of translation so far as philosophy itself is concerned, and within what limits is it possible to reduce philosophy to a language or para-language? Into which other non-natural language can one claim to translate it? These two questions go together here.

We shall answer the first with the following thesis:

Because philosophy and language are mixed together according to the principle of absolute metaphor, it is impossible to treat philosophy as one would treat a 'natural' language.

Philosophy and language—that is to say, speech—belong to each other both in fact and by right, and have done so since long before the 'linguistic turn,' yet can one conclude from this that philosophy is not only a matter of language but a medium

This essay first appeared in English translation in the fourth volume of the *Traces* book series, *Translation, Biopolitics, and Colonial Difference*, eds. Naoki Sakai and Jon Solomon (Hong Kong: Hong Kong University Press, 2006), 55-72. The topic of this volume provided the occasion for Laruelle's critical account of the philosophical concepts of biopolitics and translation, as they are found in the work of Nietzsche and Foucault.

for empirical forms of knowledge—even if only in its own fashion? Granted, philosophy's proclaimed deaths and ends allow it to subsist and to function as the common tongue stuttered by all disciplines at the end of metaphysical narratives. Has it ever been anything other than the discourse of cultures and forms of knowledge; but a unifying discourse, superior to those natural languages, which proved too Babelish? If philosophy is a language in a metaphorical sense, still more is it the superlative instance of *meta*-phor, or the *meta*-physics which internalizes languages, the universal metaphor-language, but precisely a language which bears within itself the *meta*-physical structure of *meta*-phor. Thus, it is not a mere language, or a mere linguistic metaphor of language, which would be absurd and circular, but a meta-physics of language, and hence of metaphor, a combination of metaphor (as displacement *in general* of language relative to itself) and metaphysics. This mixture amplifies one and the other, but renders the situation complex. The latter is impossible to analyze by analytical means—whatever they may be—on pain of circularity. If, in a pinch, the metaphysical can be preliminarily derived from metaphor and from the power of language, this becomes impossible and philosophy irreducible to language, and even to a usage of the latter, once the metaphysical assumes its sense and scope, which is that of being supported and swept away by the *epekeina*-phoric, or by the postulation of a real irreducible to all positing in the mode of the *meta*—as begins to become clearly perceptible with Plato, and, in fact, with every philosopher once correctly analyzed. The *epekeina*-phoric is what is most singular to philosophy, its accomplishment, and what conditions its metaphorical base in return. Strictly speaking, the essence of philosophy is mixed up with language in such a complex fashion (and on that basis, with this or that particular language) that it is obviously irreducible to a natural language and a linguistic analysis. Irreducible means here that it is not a terminological degeneration or excrescence, a reification or metastasis of language (even if it harbors such an aspect on account of its categories and transcendental terms, its governing statements, etc.), and, by the same token, that it is not amenable to logical analysis, unless it be one presupposing the prior reduction or amputation of its *epekeina*-phoric sense.

The technical concept for philosophy's supposed sufficiency as universal language or absolute metaphor, which uses natural languages in order to guarantee itself that surplus-value of translatability that the logos accords itself, is that of transcendental recursiveness.

What about the complexity of this philosophico-linguistic mixture? Philosophy is an activity of totalization rather than localization, but in the precise sense of an auto-encompassment rather than in the sense of an objectified whole. This auto-encompassment or auto-reference of philosophy is transcendental, which is to say, real in a sense that is non-empirical and constitutive of its objects. It thus pertains in all its dimensions and to all its terms, affecting them all and leaving none unperturbed.

A transcendental recursiveness is not comprehensible logically, mathematically or mechanically.

Every analysis and reduction of philosophy to such logico-analytical procedures oscillates between forgetfulness and circularity. Either it presupposes what is in question, that is to say, the possibility of such treatments, thereby 'forgetting' its object's original transcendental character; or it surreptitiously postulates a prior philosophical act granting it the right to carry out such a treatment, failing to see that if philosophy authorizes the latter, it is because it authorizes itself through such a treatment, thereby becoming self-authorizing in circular fashion.

Such logico-analytical treatments will only prove possible by way of methodological precautions and definitions of objects no longer falling within the purview of absolute metaphor but employing a language-thought that is other than philosophical.

If philosophy is absolute metaphor because it is *epekeina*-phoric (real and transcendental), this mixture is un-decomposable analytically and non-composable synthetically on the basis of philosophy and language supposed as entities 'in-themselves,' which would precisely be a particular philosophical thesis. Their reciprocal entanglement forbids a logico-linguistic analytic because every decision of this sort *about* philosophy is such that it continues to belong to the latter or is itself contaminated by transcendental auto-reference, or else falsifies its object at the very outset, or gratuitously imposes upon it a reduction of its meaning. Philosophico-linguistic hybridization is a law of the world but cannot be reproduced as such at the level of its explanation. Yet philosophy is so complex that every spontaneous logical or logico-empiricist analysis of language, even the understanding of philosophy as a *game-of* language or a *form-of*...life, remains a transcendentally recursive philosophical enterprise which merely distends philosophy, reproducing it without explaining it, like an application of absolute metaphor to itself. The hybridization of forms of knowledge is a trivial slogan and the mediocre form of this style of recursiveness. The auto-hybridization of philosophy and language under the auspices of the former is a little less so but is in reality theoretically sterile. What will be required for such objects is a procedure close to that of mixing while not repeating it in a circular fashion, a procedure that will consist in modeling the recursive mixture of philosophy and language. Every attempt at an analytic which would clarify, elucidate, or dissipate the confusions of philosophical language (from Kant's, or even Leibniz's, to Wittgenstein's) is only an attempt to purify or purge philosophical hybridization, a temptation which remains eminently...philosophical. There is an anti-philosophical reductionism that is still governed by philosophy. *This aporia must be extended to encompass every labor of logico-linguistic clarification—or even deconstruction—undertaken with respect to philosophy that would not subordinate the latter to a legitimacy superior to that of philosophy, thereby remaining subject to the latter's transcendental auto-reference.* In particular, the linguistic turn inscribes itself within the logic of this philosophical auto-reference, it remains one of the latter's particular modalities, and its innovatory scope should not be overestimated. It provided the last century with work but has only been a mode of that universal turning which philosophy as such constitutes.

Concluding thesis: The principle of translation or sufficient language, under whose auspices philosophy presents itself, remains a desire and a transcendental illusion. Thus, the problem of a universal language of translation (universal rather than communal, general, and private like philosophy) must—above all if it is to constitute a translation of philosophy—be formulated in terms other than those of philosophical recursiveness, yet with the help of the latter.

Philosophical Translation

We call 'non-philosophy' the new language, foreign to philosophy, into which we wish to translate a given philosophical discourse.

Let us consider the expression that we are making into an occasion for translation, the *biopolitics of translation*. This refers to a philosophical theory of translation, but we are in turn going to translate it into another language of thought, one that is no longer the philosophical one or a system similar to that of Nietzsche and Foucault. In other words, we must apparently invert it and formulate the problem of the *translation of the biopolitical*. Why this new project? Is it a gratuitous play on this expression? Or is it a case of rendering it intelligible and of putting forward its theory, a theory of the formulation of this expression itself? We are not going to explicate it and comment upon it as a simple 'theoretical' object but, from the outset, treat it as a particular philosophical language (that of Nietzsche and Foucault) that is simultaneously a thought. But we are going to subject this language-thought to an exercise in translation, translating it into an entirely other language-thought, one specially made for translating (and) thinking, for translating-thinking in the same gesture, which is to say, performatively, that type of language which the philosophical is. The project is not that of a 'translatology' or of a philosophy of translation, but of the translation of philosophy itself by means of a universal language.

Thus, we are transferring the problem of translation from the terrain of natural languages to that of philosophy itself. The problem concerns the object before it concerns method. Can one extend in this way the concepts of language and translation to philosophy, which presumes to take hold of the them? But from this point of view, the problem is only para-Leibnizian: it does not define an intra-philosophical theory of the translation of concepts by means of the logical or mechanical reduction of notions with a view to the constitution of a universal dictionary of 'thoughts,' or an inter-expression of doctrines. Rather, it supposes a 'non-philosophical' type of universalization of the Leibnizian project and a critique of the supposedly sufficient translato-logos which philosophy attributes to itself, as well as an equivalent universalization of the philosophical project, engendered by Foucault, of a *biopolitics of translation*, that other mode of the philosophical translato-logos. It could be said that the non-philosophical project is one concerning which philosophy displays only symptoms: a language that would finally be *genuinely* universal, endowed with concomitant powers *of translation*, *of linguistic foreignness, and of fiction*, one which would stop presupposing or simply desiring—as does the logos—that it is all these things.

The formula 'translated from the real' encapsulates philosophy; the formula 'translated from the philosophical according to the real' encapsulates non-philosophy.

What does the non-philosophical posture mean in terms of the problem of language and translation? Non-philosophy is not only a new theoretical language but a foreign language of thought, one which is practiced as the translation of a particular philosophical language or doctrine. With respect to the first point, non-philosophy harbors a non-analytic but certainly not anti-analytic program.

Philosophy posits a principle of quasi-universal translatability, the principle of sufficient translation, which governs translatology from above. But our problem does not so much concern natural languages as it concerns the translation of philosophy relative to itself—as well as between itself and its particular systems—thereby forcing us to reconsider the relation between translation and its object. The conditions for this translation of philosophy are probably of a non-translatological order and do not fall under the aegis of a philosophy of translation, which is valid for natural languages but not for translation between philosophical systems and between the forms of knowledge they mobilize. A linguistico-transcendental epistemology may settle the first case by way of operations to be carried out on languages and through the discovery of their limiting conditions, but the second uncovers a problem of an entirely different order of generality and of a different type of complexity, that of *the relation of translation to the translated itself*. What can translation do when it is examined specifically as translation of philosophy relative to itself or to empirical forms of knowledge, and relative also to the translatable and the untranslatable? What is it that is translated in non-philosophy as translation if it is not a natural language? Our problem concerns the immanence of translation's relation to its object and its cause, and what one is to understand by the 'translated,' finding out whether the latter issues from a translatable or from an untranslatable which is the cause of translation.

Non-philosophy transforms philosophy with a view to constituting itself as a language of universal translation, but at the price of a limitation of the principle of general translatability which is that of philosophy, certain nuances excepted.

It is imperative to thematize translation's philosophical conditions insofar as it is invested as a matter of fact within languages and forms of knowledge, but to do so in a non-philosophical register, or to elaborate the theory of these conditions themselves and not only gather them together. More particularly, any philosophy we select postulates, either explicitly or without knowing it, a double principle, that of the universal translatability of languages (with many nuances and obstacles excepted) and of philosophy itself into its systems; and, correlatively, that of the philosophizability of translation itself. Universal philosophizability and translatability are conjoined, without preliminary examination, in the name of a limitless increase in philosophy's own communicability and auto-legitimation. Even translatability governs translation as its principle, carrying it along and guiding it over epistemological and linguistic obstacles, or across the limits that this or that particular system believes it is laying down for translation, when it is in fact waging war against another equally particular system. *A non-philosophy will circumscribe these two principles without requisitioning local 'obstacles' or 'difficulties'* that remain circumventable and inferior for the principles in question. It will appeal instead to an instance of the real as untranslatable and more, *as without-translation, as already-translated-without-translation or as immanence (of) the translated.* And secondly, it will invoke the necessity of possessing a spontaneously practiced natural language as the basis for all philosophy, and thereby of being in possession of a condition which is necessary for philosophy but irreducible, as operative language, to the latter's two principles. The analysis of philosophizability and translatability requires the practice of a natural language which philosophy's idealism claims to sublate, internalize, and master; a practice that is positive in the manner in which a science is practiced, and which will help the real transform philosophizability and translatability into non-fundamental or non-sufficient forms. This double condition, concerning determination on the one hand, and the material or the object on the other, instantly transforms these philosophical objectives into mere principles, requirements, or desires which will remain ineffectual. The philosophizability of translation, the translatability of philosophy, will be obliged to cease in this particular form, to abandon this presumptuous type of universality and to accept more limited kinds of effective or operational realization; ones that finally provide them with objects, or oblige them to operate within the limits of experience. And here, in the context of this non-philosophical project, the limits of experience are no longer constituted by natural languages but by philosophy's *relation* to its objects and systems, a relation which we shall in turn have to relate to the real of-the-last-instance and to this reality proper to natural language as practiced—and only as practiced. The principle of sufficient translatability is equivalent to a program of philosophical foundation that a non-philosophy which would be the unified theory of philosophy, or of translatology *and* of a natural language, would come to realize or delimit through its double conditioning, thereby short-circuiting the philosophical sufficiency of translatology without eliminating the latter.

The immanence of the real, which is the already-translated, the translated-without-translation rather than the untranslatable, implies translation's unilateral or irreversible character, a conception which is obviously challenged by philosophy, for whom sufficient translatability means a translation that is possible in every direction, a recursiveness of translation.

Like mathematics, philosophy wants to be a universal interface, an operator of translation between all forms of knowledge, or, explicitly, a general language of thoughts (Leibniz), and sometimes even an absolute, rather than merely logico-mathematical, language (Hegel). To be a language for reality like this is to be a 'logos.' Thus, philosophical language is always a mechanism endowed with reciprocally convertible or inter-expressive double-faces, the linguistic turn merely constituting a supplement of convertibility for philosophy and language. Non-philosophy, by way of contrast, constitutes itself as a radical rather than absolute language, according to general conditions of determination which prize it free from philosophy as linguistico-transcendental mixture, and, initially, mixture of the real and the transcendental. It makes a secondary use of methods close to the logico-analytical register, without the positivism that the latter acquires when it becomes a philosophy in its own turn. It never constitutes a machine with two faces; it is the identity of a unilateral duality or a duality with one face, but one which has been extracted from the philosophico-linguistic complex. It is the non-logos, which is certainly not an anti-logos—but it has to be understood that the logos is the language-for-the-world. The abandonment of the logico-linguistic style, which was part of the twentieth century and its illusions, in no way implies a lack of interest in the problem of 'language' (which remains, in spite of all, a gregarious and unitary generality) and, above all, of languages, but a re-evaluation of their relations to philosophy and their meaning for the subject (of) translation.

Even the translatology that is most cautious and sensitive to obstacles and impossibilities of all types, to all the phenomena of alterity, remains in thrall to sufficient translatability. The non-philosophical conception puts translation, under the aegis of its cause and its transcendental essence, beyond the reach of the obstacles of the source language, but by the same token limits or includes within the concept of translation not only the conditions for its practical feasibility but even more so those for its effective reality. Insofar as philosophy aspires to be a universal language for regional forms of knowledge, allowing for their reciprocal translation, we do not renounce this objective but maintain that it can be attained only under non-philosophical conditions. First, it is necessary that philosophy be rendered capable of translating its own systems into one another, and thereby putting an end to their mutual incomprehension *without putting an end to their differences and, in a certain manner, to their inexchangeability*; thus, to raise 'philosophy as such' [*'la-philosophie'*], which is only a general, historico-institutional master-key, riven with permanent conflicts, to the status of an identity that would be genuinely universal or valid for all of its systems. Because philosophy is inseparable from forms of knowledge, this transformation will also be that of its relation to these forms of knowledge. Non-philosophy is that universal language-thought possessing a univocity that is no longer philosophical in kind but of-the-last-instance, into which systems and forms of knowledge can be translated, but translated into this language prior to and in order to be translated into one another.

We distinguish exchangeability or translation as encompassed within a general element that is necessarily philosophical in kind, or convertibility, which regulates this exchange, from unilateral translation, or translation by inexchangeability. 'The equivalent' (whether 'sought for' or 'general'), that favorite word of translators and economists, is a nest of question-begging assumptions and paralogisms, and harbors the most archaic of philosophical pretensions. If there is an 'equivalent' that is emergent, productive, and critical, rather than circular and conservative, it is unilateral or of-the-last-instance. As target-language, non-philosophy, by virtue of its condition of reality and in its possibility, is untranslatable into philosophical language; it is only amenable to translation on account of the material from which it draws its vocabulary and syntax. If natural languages remain difficult to convert and translatable only at the price of seizures, accidents, infelicities, and delays, one may consider philosophy at once as an attempt at smoothing them out and finally translating them, and as an enterprise that is incapable of realizing its goal since it reproduces these difficulties of translation within itself, capitalizing on them at least as much as on the benefits it accrues from this supplementary power of translation. From this point of view, non-philosophy elaborates and distributes this decision-of-translation quite differently. It limits the process of translation, eliminating—albeit only within the element of translation's cause and possibility—the mixture of its finiteness and interminability. On the other hand, it ratifies as a legitimate or a priori necessity the ambivalence of translation as terminable/interminable, but does so by restricting the pertinence of that ambivalence to the presence of the philosophico-linguistic mixture and its function as a 'material.' The decision-of-translation still exists within non-philosophy, and is even inextricable from the subject (of) translation: *the non-philosopher as existing-subject-translator*. But this decision, by way of contrast to the decision-of-translation from one language into another, is non-decisional of itself. It is determined to be of this type by a cause which has the character of a radical untranslatable, which is to say, by an identity (of the) cause of translation.

The untranslatable in the radical, as opposed to absolute, sense of the word, is neither translatable nor untranslatable in the sense in which a mixture of these two characteristics would allow. It is the real as cause-of-the-last-instance. But it would be better to say that the real is 'without-translation' (just as it is 'without-analysis'). It is for this reason, which lays low the principle of sufficient translation, that the decision (of) non-philosophical translation of the logos is carried out *according to* the without-translation-of-the-last-instance, yet opens up an infinite translatability, previously constrained or circumscribed by the principle of sufficient translation, or philosophy's terminable/interminable translatability. Generally speaking, one must, here at least, stop trying to proceed deductively from translatability's empirical conditions to its possibility, and then from the latter to its reality. It is necessary to invert, and perhaps more than invert, the causality, and proceed from the without-translation and the language to be translated, the logos, to the reality of the possibility of translating the logos itself, its systems and the forms of empirical knowledge it mobilizes.

Non-philosophical translation is 'non-Euclidean' in spirit. In the non-Euclidean approach, 'translation' is often used metaphorically, so that one speaks of the translation of one geometry into another. The inverse is possible. The bi-univocal logic of translation, even in the form of a principle of the best possible translation, of the optimal translation, which continues to presuppose a field of translations or a curve of possible equivalents for a unique term or statement, loses its pertinence in non-philosophical translation. As cause-by-immanence of translation, the without-translation suspends the coordinated mixture of quasi-infinite unicity and/or multiplicity of equivalents for a unique *traductandum*. Since it withdraws itself from the operation, it frees a unilateral duality of possibilities. On the one hand, the without-translation is more than merely the 'impossible' for translation; it excludes all translation. On the other hand, for any term taken from the logos (a doctrine, a system, a concept), it renders possible a limitless (unless it be limited by that which is finite in the philosophical material) infinity of non-philosophical translations or equivalents.

Ultimately, unilateral translation implies:

1. That non-philosophy in its essence is not translatable into the language which it translates—a thesis which is philosophically and doubtless linguistically incomprehensible.
2. That it is translatable into philosophy from the very restricted viewpoint of its material, which it constitutes for the language of translation.
3. That every system translated from philosophy into non-philosophy ceases to be translatable into another as yet untranslated system, and that it becomes so in another system only if the latter has itself been translated non-philosophically. Non-philosophy is not an inter-systemic translation but a translation-in-the-last-instance of systems as identities.

A Universal Foreign Language of Translation

Non-philosophy is specified here as unified theory of philosophy and language.

Non-philosophy contrasts with the solutions of linguistic analysis or logic of philosophy as a genuinely universal (rather than common, etc.), and thereby utterly foreign language, one needing to be learned as a foreign tongue. It does so in the specific form of a *unified theory of philosophy and language*, comprising the following aspects, which are those of a pragmatics, a theory, a foreign language, and a fiction. Philosophy corresponds to none of its aims—unless it be by way of symptoms—and still less to its means.

1. The aspect of a pragmatics, a use of philosophy for the benefit of tasks or instances that are other than philosophical, or which do not fall under the aegis of transcendental auto-reference, and which are thus immanent in a more radical fashion. Non-philosophy does not have its site in logic and language, which are for it merely instruments and materials. It constitutes a new use of philosophy, rather than its end. The death or end of philosophy, post-philosophy, etc., all presuppose a conception of the latter as auto-encompassing, in a manner excluding all possibility of its use. To propose a use of *philosophy as such* [*la philosophie*] is necessarily to relinquish its spontaneous practice, just as to program its auto-extinction is to relinquish every use of philosophy other than the intra-philosophical. Thus, non-philosophy is more than a change of function, a pragmatism internal to philosophy, or a doctrinal position. A pragmatism that has been universalized in accordance with the foundations of non-philosophy, one which is no longer a particular doctrine but instead one of the latter's postural aspects, must extend from forms of knowledge to philosophy itself, but must do so by establishing itself

as a democracy of uses and 'services.' Such a transmutation is possible only if the philosophico-linguistic complex or mixture becomes the material on the basis of which the subject as foreigner, instead of being the dispossessed claimant of that complex, now constitutes itself with the help of the latter's occasional participation.

2. The aspect of a quasi-linguistics, destined to substitute itself for that self-consciousness or spontaneous self-reference which predominates in philosophy. Non-philosophy is not a language traced from natural languages or linguistics, but a linguistics-language. Philosophy must be ushered into the realm of determinate forms of knowledge, but without being simply reduced to one of them. Philosophy is not a rigorous theory but an auto-significance, a spontaneous onto-linguistics endowed with self-consciousness or reflexiveness but no self-knowledge. *Loquor ergo sum*: this amounts to a cogito for the philosopher insofar as he or she speaks the logos; but a cogito through which he or she proves only his or her existence as spoken-speaking subject, and in no way his or her *reality* as existing-subject-translator, or his or her knowledge of the latter. This is the transcendental illusion, or even the hallucination, proper to the spoken-speaking and its sufficiency, the principle of sufficient language. The theory of 'philosophical language' has yet to be elaborated, for reasons that are not only pragmatic but primarily theoretical.

3. The aspect of a translatology developing the power of translation between forms of knowledge acquired by this unified theory or language; specifically, the concept of 'unilateral translation,' which transforms its translatological or biopolitical concept and its philosophico-linguistic presuppositions. Philosophy is a particular language precisely insofar as it parcels itself out into doctrines that are semi-private, semi-communal. It is Babel distilled to its ultimate essence, torn from

the realm of languages and transcendentalized. Philosophical Babelism goes hand in hand with philosophy's auto-referentiality and thus tries hard to disguise itself. Non-philosophy is a universal language and thus strictly *indivi-dual* or, as we will say, indivi-dual in-the-last-instance, and consequently able to treat philosophemes and doctrines, as well as forms of knowledge, as the vocabulary and grammatical rules it requires and as its means of expression. It is not a doctrine within philosophy or a system, and, from this point of view, we will distinguish a universal philosophy—a tautology devoid of effective reality—from the universality of philosophy in the mode of non-philosophy. Or again, we distinguish a future philosophy, for example a philosophy of the future, from the future of philosophy, which is a thought of the non-philosophical type, without necessarily being the latter.

4. The aspect of a foreign language, insofar as a unified or immanent language is *radically* universal and thus radically *foreign*, so that empirical forms of knowledge have to learn it in order to communicate in a way which we shall call democratic, not subjugated to communicational capital but using that language in order to liberate itself. Universal translation does not occur between natural languages, and in an ultimately reversible way between the source language and the target language, but between all of these, albeit only insofar as they support empirical forms of knowledge, and that universal and thus unilateral language which is non-philosophy. We must learn non-philosophy and make it our own as the most foreign of all languages. More precisely, the subject-speaking-non-philosophically must make philosophy his or her own, use its vocabulary and syntax with a view to manifesting him or herself as that speaking which is most radically foreign to philosophical-language, rather than to natural languages. Radical language-thought does not program the 'death' or 'end' of

the logos, whether in itself or in something else, but rather a suspension of the latter's sufficiency as language which is particular-and-total, private-and-recursive. If the logos is the superlative instance of the speaking-which-speaks, non-philosophy is the language which, on the basis of the real, speaks other-than…philosophically, the foreign-speaking-subject.

5. The aspect of a quasi-literary fiction assumed by this unification of philosophy and language; a theory rather than a fiction of universal language, but one which is capable of fictional effects. This is the idea, which is certainly difficult to put into practice, of a 'fictioning' translation [*traduction fictionnante*], or philo-fiction. Philosophy finds itself embarrassed by a terminological viscosity, a semantic motionlessness that prevents it from being fictioning [*fictionnante*] and causes it to confuse a proliferation of concepts doubling themselves specularly in proportion to their scarcity for that fictional power which produces indivi-dual clones like so many dazzling, new-born stars shining far off-shore from philosophy's spiral-nebula.

Procedures

The procedure consists in suspending the principle of sufficient language and in modeling that complex object which is absolute metaphor or the logos under the conditions of-the-last-instance of the without-translation.

1. The suspension of the principle of sufficient language, hence of philosophizability and translatability supposed as universal or merely general. *A suspension acquired in virtue of the conditions of the problem's initial formulation, and which would not have been possible or even envisageable outside the real in the radical sense of this word.* This formulation frees the philosophico-linguistic mixture from its sufficiency relative to the real, or from its sense as logos. It constitutes philosophy's real content as a supposedly 'universal' language or logos.

2. This mixture is modeled through the construction of a model that combines philosophy's transcendental power with the linguistic power of analysis in a duality-without-mixture, a duality of the 'composite' [*mixte*] that is itself the apparent aspect of the duality, this time unilateral, which the mixture forms with the real. This modeling of the logos is also acquired in its possibility and legitimacy along with—and at the very outset of—the initial formulation of the problem of a language that would be radical, immanent, and universal in accordance with the without-translation. Just as we do not from the outset reduce philosophy to the signifier or to signifying practices, we do not from the outset reduce the logos to the logico-analytical. The principle of sufficient language is much more powerful and profound than any confusions, logical or otherwise; more powerful than the lack of sense proper to metaphysical statements, or even than the logocentrism of philosophical speaking.... It is not possible to model the translato-logos without using a natural language required in an operational manner as speech and discourse, rather than as the object of a linguistics.

The translation of philosophy consists in producing a clone of the latter under the conditions of the without-translation.

Non-philosophy, considered as a thought-language, is the clone of philosophical language. The possibility of the two preceding operations is discovered in reality and in-the-last-instance as production of a clone-language obtained on the basis of the logos, and which does not replicate the latter according to the mode of philosophical auto-reference but exists in an entirely other mode, which is that of being-determined-in-the-last-instance. This language is translated from the philosophical and contains the immanent limits of a philosophizability and translatability whose universality is, in this instance, effective.

Translated from Biopolitics

Non-philosophy is a translation of the logos within the strict non-philosophical limits of the logos.

A 'biopolitics of translation' implies so many philosophical presuppositions that it is incorporated, as we have already stated, into our problematic as a particular doctrine which we must, in turn, 'translate' into non-philosophical language. But *the passage from the biopolitics of translation to the (non-philosophical) translation of biopolitics* is only apparently an inversion. For this kind of translation is a limitation of the philosophizability and translatability implied in the expression 'biopolitics,' and a 'realization' or 'effectuation' of the latter precisely within the limits of a non-philosophical experience of the philosophy encapsulated in this expression. It is carried out in the form of a redefinition of life, of the translator-subject, of translation, and lastly of the expression's universal scope.

Translated into non-philosophical language-thought, 'life' ceases to be intertwined with the operation of translation and determines it without reciprocity.

Nietzsche and Foucault posit a production of life by translation at worst, a reciprocal determination of life and translation at best. But as immanent life which says or names the real without determining it, life is now such that it determines translation instead. We transform the occasional expression or language-thought (the logos) 'the biopolitics of translation' into another language-thought, and do so on the spot, or in an immanent fashion, from the point of view of practice as well as from the point of view of that 'language-thought' whose immanence renders it indivisible in its terms. This is a translation that constitutes the theory or explanation for this occasional expression, and which, with the same terms and on the basis of their philosophical relations, reveals another experience of life and translation, in the form of statements with an axiomatic and theorematic aspect. Nothing could be further from a doctrine opposing itself to that of 'the biopolitics of translation' (a language does not oppose itself to another), or from the description of a previously unnoticed state of affairs. The practice of language-thought is henceforth immanent and only describes objects and acts from within the bounds of an axiomatic apparatus.

Life as lived (of) translation, as another first name for the real, is strictly undivided without forming a totality. It would be better to say that the lived of translation is immanent or lived-in-lived and without-the-operation-of-life. Of course, this is the without-translation or the without-logos rather than the 'untranslatable,' and, as a result, it determines translation and its operations only in-the-last-instance, taking them into consideration without alienating itself in them, bringing them forth into the new language-thought without relating to them, thereby transforming them into elemental hybrids without intertwining itself with them to form those mixtures that philosophers set out to unravel while in fact busily rebinding them and rendering them ever more indissoluble.

The lived (of) translation implies the 'dualysis' (the unilateral duality) of the 'biopolitical' theme as duality of the immanent lived or lived-without-life and the subject (of) translation.

Such a subject exists, and only exists, as translator, and even only as translation of a language-thought into one which is entirely other, that is to say, it exists as system of operations assumed in-the-last-instance in the mode of a radical lived. There is no already-given subject 'behind' the operations of non-philosophical translation (reductions, modeling, cloning); the subject constitutes itself or *exists* within the immanence of cloning as assumption of these operations by the lived. The latter thereby raises or abstracts an existing-subject-translator in which it does not lose itself precisely because it does not alienate itself in it, rendering it instead heteronomous to the source language which, however, it uses as subject.

The translator exists for-language or is in-struggle against communicational capital.

The translator thereby changes in function and in status. To exist is to translate the philosophical into the non-philosophical, but translation does not exhaust the lived, which nothing exhausts or which is foreclosed to the very act of translation. Although one can say 'I translate therefore I am,' it is impossible to proceed deductively from translation to the real, only to being or life, but not to that which is radically lived. The metaphysical subject is also translated into an existing-subject-translator, it has lost its transcendental illusion, the narcissism or sufficiency generally concomitant with the target-language, but which are now for us those of the source-language. Yet, in virtue of this very fact, the subject has been constituted-in-the-last-instance as 'turned' *toward* the source or original language, for the benefit of the latter and for its salvation.

What is a translator for if not granting full meaning to the communication of idioms, as though it constituted their very salvation? One must distinguish two movements belonging to each other, but in a relation of unilateral duality. Doubtless, on the one hand, a movement consisting in the accumulation of communicational capital and which the biopolitics of translation, and the translation of natural languages in general, necessarily ensures. But on the other hand, a movement consisting in the de-capitalization, if not of the lived, then of the subject's life or existence at least, which is to say, the salvation effected through the language-thought par excellence, the one which turns all other thoughts and languages into language-thoughts the moment it translates them through unilateral translation.

The non-philosophical translator has as his or her task to ensure the salvation of the logos outside its auto-enslavement.

The translating-subject exists-as-foreigner [*existe-Etranger*] in a relation of struggle with philosophical language, not on account of the latter, but through its lived-without-translation. Being-in-philosophical language [*L'être-à-la-langue philosophique*] is now no more than a material for a translation that is *for* the latter or *for* the philosophical as such [*le-philosophique*] as world-language. The biopolitics of translation was a concern for language accompanied by a simultaneous or reversible concern for the subject, a discipline producing the being of the subject. But a more radical 'subjective' use of the logos is possible, a pragmatics harboring a therapeutic care or concern only insofar as it transforms the latter into the salvation of the world-language from its appearances.

Non-philosophy is the non-Adamic language-thought.

Non-philosophy as universal language-thought may appear to be an attempt at philosophical, and in this instance translatological, deprogramming. Might it be an Adamic language, one that has been revealed to men? Not in the sense of an originary and historically primary language. Non-philosophical language presupposes only its material; only the language to be translated as revealed to subjects since it is given to them externally in the shape of philosophy. But the latter is precisely what must be transformed as existing-subject-translation. Non-philosophical language is primary in the sense in which priority is now devoid of the primacy of the real. It is transcendental rather than empirico-linguistic. Ultimately, it is more than originary, it is uni-originary through its cause and archi-originary through its transcendental essence, real-in-the-last-instance. Is there a double language? No, there is a single source with numerous species: the philosophical, and a certain regime or pragmatics of this idiom. Language-thoughts are ‘two’ only in the form of a unilateral duality. Ultimately, non-philosophical language is universal in a radical mode. ‘Universal’ languages are either of the creationist or the artificial type, the former functioning all too well but forgotten, the latter not functioning at all. As for those cobbled-together [*bricolées*] technological languages, they immediately increase the stockpile of communicational capital, and are merely international rather than universal.

Chapter 5

A New Presentation of Non-Philosophy

Translated by Ray Brassier

Let me begin in traditional terms: what is the essence, what are the possibilities of non-philosophy? From the outset, it originated from four concerns that were coupled two by two; and hence from dualities. It continued to develop in terms of dualities, constantly calling them into question but never dispensing with them entirely. Its current possibilities or themes are merely a continuation or development of this (non-)essence…

> …Thus, my point of view here will be historical and systematic. This reconstruction after the fact cannot avoid appearing to be a piece of retrospective self-interpretation, but since fidelity here is not to a historically predetermined meaning or truth, but to a last instance, and hence to the spirit of dualities, I stop short of anything that could draw us into a hermeneutics.

This text is a translation of a lecture delivered in French at the Middlesex University Department of Philosophy in November, 2003. The ellipses and indented paragraphs indicate pauses, asides, and interjections within the flow of the larger presentation. The French text, along with the English translation, appeared on the ONPhi website (www.ONPhi.net) in February, 2004.

The genealogy of non-philosophy is problematic. Born, like everything else, of the intersection between two original and loosely coupled problems—whose coupling was not quite as arbitrary as the encounter between *Poros* [Expediency] and *Penia* [Poverty][1]—non-philosophy has always refused to be their synthesis, and hence their offspring. Philosophy was born of the one-sided encounter between a sleeping being (Poros) and the desire for a child (Penia), but as a philosopher Plato ultimately remains beholden to biology—he does not get right to the bottom of Poros' sleep, because he still attributes it to drunkenness and closed eyes, to a merely slumbering intelligence. Similarly, he does not get right to the bottom of Penia's poverty, because he still attributes her desire for a child to her *sighting* of Poros. Plato does not go beyond the *pharmakon* as coupling, as condition for the couple or procreation.

This filiation is not that of non-philosophy. Like every child, she consents to be born according to biological conditions, but she refuses the continuity of birth; she is an orphan and it is she who decides to be born 'according to X.' She sees in the drunkenness of her father merely the symptom of man's blindness, of an un-learned knowing; and sees in her mother's desire for a child the symptom of the impossible desire for being-blind. Not refusing the past, but refusing to be determined by it, presenting herself as the daughter of man, her problem is that of being and remaining ahead of the image of the newborn. It is in this simply human manner that she escapes from the biological and familial cycle and provides—without founding a new family or some sort of new city—the basis-in-person for a new type of organization: an organization of heretics, of sons or daughters of man who are continuously newborn, grateful orphans of philosophy and the world. As for the act of birth,

1. Cf. Plato, *Symposium*, 203, b-c. –Tr.

whereas philosophy is destined to parricide and is only capable of acknowledging its filiation through this founding crime, non-philosophy tries to avoid the synthesis of expediency and poverty that is parricide. Born according to X, which is to say, according to man as the unknown, non-philosophy joins its parents to the city of brothers and sisters, elevating its own filiation to utopian status.

In actuality, the structure (but not the origin) of non-philosophy consists of a principal duality and a secondary duality. The principal duality is the following:

1. The enigmatic character of the One, of its essence, its origin; the fact that it is forgotten and subordinated to Being. The Heideggerian preoccupation with Being and the Lacanian and Derridean preoccupation with the Other rendered this forgetting of the One more crucial, as though the circle of philosophy had not been fully covered in its entirety. Philosophy continuously talked about the One, presupposed it, invoked it, but without properly thematizing it.
2. There was another kind of forgetting in the guise of philosophy's abusive attitude, its abuse of power in general; the way in which it laid claim to reality and truth, but also to domination; the arbitrary nature of its questioning. How was such a form of thinking possible? One that claimed to be undeniable without furnishing any credentials other than its own practice and tradition, rather like an unfounded and interminable rumor?

So, on the one hand an entity that reigns without governing: the One; and on the other a discipline that claims to provide a theoretical domination of the world and of other forms of thought to such an extent that it presumes to have a proprietary claim on 'thinking.' I found myself faced with a new and apparently artificial duality, since in normal circumstances the One was, after all, merely an object of philosophy. But this duality was accompanied by another, which seemed to graft itself upon it necessarily, as though it provided the means for realizing it. This was the duality of science and philosophy, which I have up until now tended to privilege as a guiding thread when recapitulating the history of non-philosophy, and which continues to hold sway in the idea of non-philosophy as a discipline. There is a sense in which I have never exited from this space, from its type of duality and internal unity; even if, as I hope to show, it has undergone contractions and expansions—and above all redistributions. My problem was never that of the One and the multiple, even if I often evoked it. But in non-philosophy one must be wary of confusing the object with which one struggles, and the essence of the struggle, the former frequently occluding the latter. My problem has been that of the One and the two, in the sense in which the two is something specific and not synonymous with the multiple. My problem has to do with a tradition that differs from, or is parallel to, that of philosophy. It has to do with the struggle with philosophy. It is a transcendental mathematics, but one that will have to abandon the Platonic or philosophical form of transcendental numbers, and stop being a divine mathematics (Leibniz). Thus, it is a struggle on twice two fronts: that of the One and that of the two, that of the definition of philosophy and that of science. This makes at least four fronts. This quadripartite structure of the struggle is the dimension within which I have confronted another quadripartite, the one constituted by the philosophers who 'influenced' me, as they say. When reconstructing the history of non-philosophy, I have often confused this second quadripartite with the first, committing a category mistake by according it an excessive influence, when in fact it was already no more than the material for the first, or a terrain for the struggle. These problems were resolved as I came to understand that instead of trying to unify these four sides philosophically by binding or suturing them together in a relational exteriority, I could do so through another kind of unity, one effected through a radically immanent cloning. As a result, the notions of 'struggle' and 'front' undergo a transformation. What was required was a unilateral leap, which is to say, abandoning all pretension on the side of the One, no longer positing it as one of the sides or terms of the quadripartite, acknowledging its collapse or non-consistency. This meant giving up at the same time the idea of a 'head-to-head' struggle and elaborating the notion of a *unilateral front*. That every struggle engages two fronts but only puts one combatant into play was a riddle that was resolved when it turned into its own solution. This involves a shift from the divine logos to a practice placed under the name-of-man.

> The problematic of the quadripartite, of its binding or cloning, has the advantage of allowing a synoptic overview of all the stages—even the most rudimentary—in the research that led to non-philosophy, and of not dismembering it in terms of historical distinctions. Before being non-philosophical, the magma from which non-philosophy emerged has all the characteristics of a pre-philosophical *chôra*, from its deepest to its most superficial layer, like a landmass or conglomerate rising up when the tectonic plates underlying the philosophical continent start breaking up. The division of non-philosophy intro three stages privileges a historical overview and should be inscribed within the structure of the quadripartite.

I will confine myself here to sketching an outline and drawing a continuous guiding thread for the development of non-philosophy, while passing over two kinds of circumstance that played a part in and affected this development. On the one hand, the innumerable hesitations, misgivings, amendments and variations in the binding of these two terms. For in the beginning it was a question—as it is for every philosopher—of identifying the point of suture between the two sides of this duality, which philosophy had summarily realized or admitted in the form of systems and their traditions. On the other hand, there were the personal conditions under which non-philosophy existed, adverse institutional circumstances, all sorts of phantasms, various interests that exceeded the bounds of philosophy alone—these do not need to be recalled here since we are trying to identify a structure and the history contained within it.

For the moment, it is still a question of binding rather than of cloning. These dualities were already present in the initial series of works grouped together under the heading *Philosophy I*, but were still being resolved to the benefit of the side of philosophy and binding, and to the detriment of the One and science. The shift to *Philosophy II* occurs by way of an overturning: it is now the One which becomes the principal theme and assumes the mantle of the real, and philosophy that is evaluated in terms of the One's capacity for being conceived 'for itself' and as such, or as immanent. This is the gist of *Le principe de minorité*[2]. However…

2. *Le principe de minorité* [The Minority Principle] (Paris: Aubier, 1981). –Ed.

...Non-philosophy does not effectively or successfully begin until *Une biographie de l'homme ordinaire*[3], because it is there that the problem of how to bind the four sides together is thematized and basically formulated—albeit not without difficulties—through the notion of unilaterality. The conditions for this solution are that the One acquire a radical autonomy with regard to philosophy, that it stop being a philosophical object, and that the latter is revealed to be a transcendental appearance. It is as though an over-neo-Platonization of the One were accompanied by a corresponding over-Kantianization of philosophy as appearance...

> ...Formulated in this way, without satisfying the pretensions of philosophy vis-à-vis the One, the problem increased in difficulty. We had deprived ourselves of every philosophical solution. Nevertheless...

...The germ of the solution resided in this excessive separation between the One and philosophy, which amounted to a sort of Platonic *chorismos*. In effect, the cause of their exteriority or reciprocal autonomy, and hence of their unity, could no longer be philosophical or one that operated through transcendence. Moreover, the One in question was no longer *epekeina*-physical, or beyond being, so that, on the contrary, what caused this

3. *Une biographie de l'homme ordinaire: Des Autorités et des Minorités* [*A Biography of the Ordinary Man: Of Authorities and Minorities*] (Paris: Aubier, 1985). Laruelle has divided his work after *Philosophy I* and *II* into two additional phases, *Philosophy III* and *IV*. The shift to *Philosophy III* and beyond is, in part, the subject of the present chapter, which describes how non-philosophy, rather than just functioning as a science or discipline of philosophy, can be a unified theory of philosophy in its various relations to (and last-instance identity with) science and other forms of knowledge. For more on the phases of the non-philosophy project, see *Principes de la non-philosophie* (Paris: PUF, 1996). –Ed.

separation had to be its radical immanence. But how could radical immanence be reconciled with exteriority?

> At this stage, as my path momentarily crossed that of Michel Henry, the other half of the problem remained unresolved—specifically: how could one still use philosophy—which was not designed for this end—to speak of this One or radical immanence? The initial project of a theoretical domination of philosophy and of a critique of its transcendental appearance reappeared in a new form: that of the transformation of philosophical statements or phrases. This was the idea of a theoretical discipline with philosophy as its object. All of *Philosophy I* and a large part of *Philosophy II* are devoted to a twofold task: On the one hand, to a more and more precise binding of the duality which is outside every system or synthesis by combining three requirements: that of the One's radical immanence; that of the unilaterality of this duality; and finally that of the reduction of the logos to the status of a structured appearance or material. On the other hand, to the search for a discourse that would no longer be the logos and whose resources (despite this discourse being appropriated by the causality of the One) would be provided by philosophy alone; thus, to the constitution of a discipline of philosophy in view of thinking the One.
>
> But to present non-philosophy in this way, in terms of a problem of binding, is to tip the scale in favor of philosophy once again—albeit philosophy as the object of a discipline. It may be that this is a step forward. And I admit that it is possible to freeze the development of non-philosophy at one or other of its stages, so long as

> its essential conditions of existence are acknowledged. I believe much of the work that will be presented to you today develops this aspect and this concept of non-philosophy as a rigorous discipline of philosophy—an aspect which, let me repeat once more, is very real. Nevertheless, there is obviously the risk of an excessive formalization of the rules governing this practice, in the manner of a universally recognizable corpus guaranteeing a certain epistemological coherence…

…Non-philosophy is neither a universal method taking over from deconstruction, nor an immanent process in which method and material, rational and real, are fused together, as in Hegel. Everything depends on how unilaterality binds—if I may be allowed to continue using this term—the opposing terms. Although non-philosophy has a *disciplinary aspect*, it is not just another discipline.

For it is in fact the other side, that of the One, that must, by definition, have primacy over philosophy from the outset, and it is according to it that one should unilaterally balance or unbalance the quadripartite as a whole. The One is not just the condition of possibility for non-philosophy—this formulation is too Kantian and empirico-idealist. It is however its *presupposed*, and as such is not once more in the service of philosophy. Unlike a condition or presupposition, which disappears into the conditioned, the presupposed has an autonomy that is irreducible to the conditioned. Whence the necessity of developing this side of the One so as to turn it into, if not the center, then at least the principal aspect of non-philosophy. In fact, the essential gains, those that condition the theory, were made on the side of the One—not the One alone, but precisely this logic of unilaterality which goes together with the One and its immanence. And it so happens that the successful adjustment of the second duality—that of philosophy and science—depends on the kind of solution one has found for the first.

How is one to re-establish the structure's *unilateral equilibrium*? Unilaterality should no longer be understood in a Hegelian sense as abstraction of one side at the expense of the other. It has to be understood as a formulation close to two others used by contemporary philosophers. It is similar to (1) 'no-relation' in Lacan's 'there is no sexual relation.' The real in Lacan as well as in non-philosophy is without relation in the sense that it excludes symbolic and linguistic relation. It is generally foreclosed to relation, as is required by radical immanence or the fact that, as Lacan says, the real always comes back to 'the same place.' It is also similar to (2) 'relation-without-relation' in Derrida, who puts the absence of relation or the Other who is without relation at the heart of relation, i.e. the logos. In other words, Lacan and Derrida are moved by antithetical motives with regard to the real: the former wants to exclude all relation, while the latter is content to differentiate relation through its other and hopes to find the real in an affect of absolute Judaic alterity. Their difference can be situated between two conceptions of the Other, but it does not basically touch on the real. Both conceive of the 'without-relation' in the same way: the former (Lacan) as opposed to relation, or as non(-relation); the latter (Derrida), more subtly, as at the very least indissociable from relation. In either case, psychoanalysis or deconstruction, *relation is presupposed as that in terms of which the real must be posited*. And relation is transcendence or a certain kind of exteriority. Both cases remain within the realm of philosophy and seek immanence, the without-relation, through opposition or in terms of an ultimate reference to transcendence. Under these conditions, the real cannot be radically relationless, even in Lacan, where the real and the symbolic are linked through topology. Can one follow Lacan but go beyond Lacan by positing a real that is de-symbolized, un-chained from the signifier, unconditioned by it; yet one which, as in Derrida, nevertheless continues to have a proven effect on the logos or symbolic realm in general?

What I have called *unilaterality* is the solution-without-synthesis to this problem. It is the only kind of relation tolerated by the real as immanence and primacy over philosophy. On the one hand, it is essentially a radical non-relation, as in Lacan—but one which is genuinely radical this time because its non-relationality follows from its immanence. More than ever, the real returns to the same place, to such an extent that it no longer defines one and is u-topic through and through. But on the other hand, it does not remain alone because it is separated (from) the logos or the world—it is also an Other, but without relation to transcendence, which would otherwise continue to define it and constitute it. It is other-*than*…relation, rather than other *to*…relation, whether as opposed to it (Lacan), or partially internalized by it (Derrida). There is an alterity that goes with the One but is itself One or radical immanence. *There is no longer an Other of the Other as there necessarily is in psychoanalysis and philosophy*. This is why I use the term 'unilation' instead of the word 'relation.' This is the place of the non-philosophical concept of unilaterality: between Hegel, who reduces it to an abstraction of the understanding; Lacan, who ultimately does not understand it and tolerates it only in order to cancel it in the signifying chain through which he thinks he acknowledges it; and Derrida and others, who try to grant it a status but one that remains within the realm of philosophical exteriority. The radical has primacy over the unilateral, but primacy is not itself a relation.

More concretely, consider a philosophical system, i.e. a dyad of terms that are opposed or correlated through a

> third term which is itself divided between an immanent or transcendental One and a One that transcends the dyad. We move to a unilateral duality in the following way. The One is no longer divisible into real and transcendental, it is real and takes the place of one and only one term in the dyad: it now constitutes one of the two terms as indivisible and is simply immanent to the new duality. But the status of the second term in the dyad is also immediately transformed. It is no longer face-to-face with the One, which is immanent even from the perspective of this second term, and yet it exists and makes up a duality with the One without being face-to-face with it; hence without entering into relation with it. We will say that this second term is also in-One or immanent even though it is expelled from the One, which it does not constitute. More precisely, we will say that *it is expelled only insofar as the One is radically separate from what it gives or manifests*. This is why I continue to repeat that philosophy, which is the second term, is given in a radically immanent fashion or in the mode of the One, even as it is expelled from the One…

…The unilateral duality excludes the two major types of traditional solution: the theory of relations and the theory of judgments. It is not a relation, whether internal or external, and it is not a judgment, whether analytic or synthetic. It is precisely because it has none of the characteristics of a system that non-philosophy, which excludes synthesis as well as analysis, possesses the quasi- or non-analytic power of systems and their subsets, as well as the quasi- or non-synthetic power of the systems which it brushes up against in each of their points. We use the term 'dualysis' to designate this activity carried out through unilateral dualities, which analyze without an operation of analysis and synthesize without an operation of synthesis. Non-philosophical statements are neither contained analytically within those of philosophy nor added synthetically to them. It is not a matter of complex judgments and interpretation, but of transformation through the force of unilaterality.

> Unilaterality proceeds through two stages. The first is that of the real, whose immanence is no longer that of a punctual, still transcendent interiority, but a being-separate from what it expels, or rather that which it is separated from. The second is transcendental and takes this other term into account. It relates to philosophy, which, expelled-in-One, so to speak, now calls for help from the real. In the first phase, there is already duality, but on the basis of the One and its primacy: the second term is mentioned without yet being referred to. In the second phase, duality is explicitly present but on the basis of philosophy—although it does not go so far as to constitute a two.

The immanence of the One and the transcendence proper to philosophy are now so tightly and intimately bound together that there is no longer any relation but only an alterity of the One, which is an immanence without relation to philosophy—even though it gives or manifests philosophy while separating itself from it…

> …The work undertaken since the book on non-Marxism[4] has sought to carry out this intimate binding of the two sides and to justify the discipline devoted to philos-

4. *Introduction au non-marxisme* (Paris: PUF, 2000). –Ed.

ophy through the primacy and unilaterality of the One.

Thus, as I have already said, I accept that it may be necessary to isolate aspects or moments of non-philosophy in order to examine them, or even—why not—develop them into independent disciplines. Nevertheless, one should bear in mind non-philosophy's indivisible duality, the fact that it is structured in phases, so as not to separate in an abstract fashion the One from philosophy, and vice versa. But we have seen why this indivisibility or intimacy of non-philosophy is not that of a system. The truth is that we find ourselves here at the heart of the non-philosophical solution. By striving to bind and suture together opposed terms, we are forced to realize not only that that they were not really opposed, but that *they are not bound together* and that the genuinely guiding problematic for us may not be philosophical—we have been trying to prize it free from philosophy piece by piece. Non-philosophy, which began as a problem of binding, unbinding and rebinding, is radically fulfilled as something that we could never have imagined, since we were deceived by the exteriority of philosophy. It is fulfilled as a cloning. If all philosophy comes down to a question of binding, non-philosophy comes down to a question of cloning, which is *also* the answer to the question of binding. The One gives its identity to philosophy precisely insofar as the latter refuses it—an identity which philosophy both refuses and requires. We could say—parodying Lacan's famous formula about love by inverting it in favor of the giver rather than the receiver—that *the One withholds itself, thereby giving itself to philosophy, which requires it by refusing it.* If non-philosophy attains a point of unilateral equilibrium, of fulfillment proper to it, it is through this inversion of binding into its point of immanence, which is not a dead-end but rather the point at which there is a radical interiorization of the real and an inversion of philosophy. A bind forms a point of immanence, but its principle is not radical immanence—it is rather a combination of the two, through topology for example. I spent a long time looking for such a point: the point of the cogito, the point of Nietzschean transmutation, the point of critique. Non-philosophy may well be philosophy's critical point, but it is not critique that makes the point; it is the 'point' that critiques. I consider this long hunt for immanence to have reached its goal when immanence gives itself as and through a unilateral leap—that of the (non-)One, which is the key to the hunt. Cloning assembles and retroactively legitimates all those hesitant investigations, all those contradictory hypotheses about the problem of the theory's internal coherence.

Consequently, with regard to philosophy there was, strictly speaking, no overturning but rather a displacement. But a displacement without an operation can only be a utopia. And what is displaced is philosophy as such, because displacement here resolves itself into an 'en-placement.' There is no non-philosophical gesture, just the leap or unilateral operation whereby human utopia affects every possible site and frees or furnishes a 'space' for the subject.

> It will be objected that binding is more intelligible than cloning. But these solutions are neither opposed nor complementary. The real difficulty with this objection is that binding is not straightforwardly and uniquely mathematical but also transcendental, and that such a combination, which is difficult because it is an internalized topology, is precisely what calls for the solution of unilateral duality in which cloning takes binding as its object. This is what explains the possibility of taking philosophy as object for a real that does not objectify it, but transforms it.

Non-philosophy is obviously not a theory of knowledge or a system in general. It is a real-transcendental science of the world. The only way of discovering it is by relativizing the exclusive primacy of the logic that hides it and prevents one noticing it in philosophy, even of the non-analytical kind. We could say, in our customary style, that it is a transcendental logic that is real-and-nothing-but rather than logical; one that is *without-logic or non-formal*, so to speak. Contrary to the logicist reduction of philosophy, which leaves the hidden prerogatives of philosophical sufficiency intact, specifically in the form of positivity and hence of a kind of dogmatism, this non-philosophical reduction of philosophy is at once real-transcendental and capable of a wide variety of realizations, not only in terms of logic but in terms of the sciences in general. There is an instance that is more radical than logic, and this is the real. Not that it is possible to replace logic by just any science while maintaining the same privileges for the latter. It is the universal posture of science that must take the place which in philosophy is held by the restricted universality of logic. Non-philosophy shatters the strictures of logic and analytical reduction, just as it dissolves the residues of a compulsory, exclusive and primary logic in the transcendental logic of philosophers, granting the transcendental the sole support of the radical real, and hence the possibility of entering into combination with each of the sciences. Non-philosophy is *unified theory*: a radical extension of philosophy beyond transcendental logic, but one that deprives it of its traditional pretensions. As a result, it is philosophy and its logical organon that lose their prerogatives by being turned into a simply real-transcendental organon.

Thus, it is necessary to take the expression 'non-philosophy' quite literally, so to speak. It is not just a metaphorical reference to 'non-Euclidean.' It is possible for the One and the (non-)One to be identical because we are no longer operating in the realm of transcendence. Nothingness is transcendent but the *non-* is the One in all its immanent unilaterality. Non-philosophy is the inversion of philosophy; it is the *non-* addressed to philosophy by man, who is the presupposed that philosophy cannot get rid of. It is not that there is philosophy first, which then has to be denied—philosophy is given from the outset as suspended in the future by the future, and this is the determining condition for its becoming the object of a new discipline.

As for the trilogy of real, philosophical material, and unilateral syntax (or determination-in-the-last-instance), to which non-philosophy is often reduced, there is a sense in which it bears a marked resemblance—despite the difference in content—to the Lacanian triad Real-Symbolic-Imaginary, and like the latter, it is merely a structural base for non-philosophy. I, too, could say, like Lacan, that the latter is not an all-purpose grid, but rather a sort of *vade-mecum*, dangerous to the extent that it traces the structure of the philosophical system by simply distorting it. It has to be said that this trilogy was placed at the head of ONPhI[5] in the form of three axioms so as to allow the latter's constitution and functioning, but at the cost of a certain approximation and the risk of encouraging a new kind of scholastic common sense or formalism. A large part of my research has been devoted to putting this trilogy into practice and extending it to new materials. But the principal task has been trying to achieve a parallel adjustment of these instances so as to bring them all into play; tuning and adjusting the in-

5. Organisation Non-philosophique Internationale (www.ONPhi.net). –Tr.

strument; coordinating and recalibrating the apparatus. ONPhI was constructed like an un-tuned instrument, in which everyone wants to play their part with the instrument they have cobbled together themselves, preferring a free interpretation of the axioms to their free effectuation. There is a fundamental problem concerning the articulation of these three instances. Two tasks need to be carried out. The new articulation of the three terms will have to (1) undo their topological and hence structural organization, overcome the appearance that they are three by showing how they are each time two, and that each of these two is ultimately 'one' while remaining 'two' from the viewpoint of one of them; (2) define boundaries or degrees of freedom in the 'preparation' of this apparatus, but in a way that does not end up destroying it.

In any case, non-philosophy did not invent 'the real,' or the One, or man (every philosopher can take some credit for the latter), or even the idea of a 'radical immanence' (there is Michel Henry and perhaps others as well—Maine de Biran? Marx?). On the other hand, non-philosophy exists because it invented the true characteristics of the latter, because it took the requirements of radicality seriously and distinguished between the radical and the absolute. It has had to carry out a complete overhaul of the entire philosophical apparatus even when it seemed closest to it. These characteristics are:

1. The full sense of immanence as real 'before' it assumes a transcendental function.
2. The necessity of treating immanence through immanence, rather than through a transcendent overview. It is at once a structure and an immanent knowing of this structure, or what I call 'the vision-in-One.'
3. Philosophy's being already given in-One, its unilation rather than external relation to the real.

4. The structure of real immanence as unilaterality, unilateral (duality), as other than… or alterity through immanence, rather than as a metaphysical point.
5. The coupling of real determination and determination-in-the-last-instance or transcendental determination (cloning), and the thesis that Marx's concept provides a symptom of the latter.
6. The unilateral duality of man and of the subject as function, with the world as free variable.
7. The discovery of radical immanence or unilaterality as human Messianism or immanent future, its vocation for utopia and fiction.
8. The two aspects of the future language spoken by non-philosophical subjects: axiomatic or mathematical, and philosophical or oracular.

Non-philosophy is a human mathematics—a formulation I would oppose to Leibniz's conception of philosophy as a 'divine mathematics.' Radicality should be understood in terms of these principles or modes of operation, which prevent one from mistaking it for the radicality invoked by Descartes or Husserl. Everything can be summed up in terms of the distinction between the radical and the absolute.

Lastly, a few words about these new possibilities.

Non-humanist. With topological binding, philosophy remained in the hands of a *deus ex machina*: the philosopher or infant-king, who surveys and arranges the former like a handyman assembling and destroying scale models of worlds, or a demon whispering answers to Socrates. With cloning, it is finally man and man alone who is implicated in philosophy. But man is not implicated in the way being is implicated as bound up with the question of Being. Man is the real or the answer, the minimal but insufficient condition necessary for local resolutions. Non-philosophy is the primacy of man as non-immanent over being and nothingness. It is to man and man alone, not to matter or religion, that it falls to reduce humanism, for example, along with the problems of which humanism is symptomatic. Non-philosophy is the discovery that man is determining, and that he is determining-in-the-last-instance as subject.

Non-theological. Insofar as man gives the world while remaining separate from it—but not separate as an exception to it—non-philosophy invalidates all metaphysical problems such as that of the creation, procession, emanation, or conversion of the world—the entire philosophical dramaturgy. Man is a grace for the world. This is an inversion of the philosophies of transcendence and of the divine call addressed to man, because it is now the world that calls on man. Where philosophy knows the exception, non-philosophy knows—dare I say it—the miracle, but one that has been mathematized, shorn of its theological transcendence.

Non-historical. The immanent One-real is also given as other than…or separated; as the future that precedes the past and the present. Man is not consciousness, he is the force of utopia or of immanent Messianism that accompanies his confrontation with the world and inverts every possible course of history. Nietzsche's overhuman 'yes' has to be included in the 'no' that accompanies man from the depth of his immanence.

Non-literary. Non-philosophy is an activity of fiction both in thought and language; it crowns the discipline of philosophical theory. New terms should surge forth from the non-philosophical understanding in the way essences surge forth from the divine understanding according to Leibniz. They should combine the enigmatic authority of the oracle with the clarity of the theorem.

Ultimately, I see non-philosophers in several different ways. I see them, inevitably, as subjects of the university, as is required by worldly life, but above all as related to three fundamental human types. They are related to the analyst and the political militant, obviously, since non-philosophy is close to psychoanalysis and Marxism—it transforms the subject by transforming instances of philosophy. But they are also related to what I would call the 'spiritual' type—which it is imperative not to confuse with 'spiritualist.' The spiritual are not spiritualists. They are the great destroyers of the forces of philosophy and the state, which band together in the name of order and conformity. The spiritual haunt the margins of philosophy, gnosticism, mysticism, and even of institutional religion and politics. The spiritual are not just abstract, quietist mystics; they are *for* the world. This is why a quiet discipline is not sufficient, because man is implicated in the world as the presupposed that determines it. Thus, non-philosophy is also related to gnosticism and science-fiction; it answers their fundamental question—which is not at all philosophy's primary concern: "*Should humanity be saved? And how?*" And it is also close to spiritual revolutionaries such as Müntzer and certain mystics who skirted heresy. When all is said and done, is non-philosophy anything other than the chance for an effective utopia?

Chapter 6

Identity and Event

Translated by Ray Brassier

To think means, for example, to think the event; but how does thinking itself become an event? And what kind of event? The immediate empirical and philosophical characteristics used to describe the event are well known—I will not discuss them here since my concern is rather with articulating the conditions for a rigorous theory of the event. A theory of the event presupposes two operations that are probably unified, but certainly not (for reasons we will see below) reciprocal. The first operation consists in foregrounding the intra-philosophical invariants for every thinking of the event, thereby revealing how the most general structure of philosophy is condensed within the event as such, so that philosophy becomes the prototype condensing 'eventality' [*l'événementialité*]; the figure par excellence of the event—this is 'the philosophy-event,' which I will call the world-event, for I postulate that philosophy is the form of the world.

The second is very different and consists in determining the type of thought that is able to take this philosophy or world-event as its object, and in putting forward the type of real or

This essay was first published in English translation in *Pli: The Warwick Journal of Philosophy* 9 (2000), 174-189. The English text appeared on the ONPhi website (www.ONPhi.net) in June, 2003.

instance able to assume the role of cause for this thought. At both stages, identity will be at issue. In the first, as One-Other or supreme instance of philosophy (the object of the *epekeina tes ousias*).[1] In the second, as One-in-One or One that is no longer also Other, no longer measurable relative to essence, but is rather without-essence, to the extent that it is no longer even 'beyond essence.' This is what I call the real.

From the Philosophy of the Event to the Philosophy-Event or World

I will first bring to the fore a certain philosophical 'logic' of the event, a logic conditioning every figure of the event, to the extent of rendering this logic itself the event par excellence. The event's philosophical conditions of possibility are self-evident. But what is less evident is to show that these conditions exhaust all of philosophy as such and that philosophy is the prototype of the event. Consider: the event has become a theme that allows one to gather and situate almost all of French philosophy after the period of structuralism in its strict sense: it is apparently post-metaphysical and post-historical. But conversely, to what extent do these philosophies of the event constitute an event that is itself historical and philosophical?

My hypothesis is that those philosophies of history that postulated a certain homogeneity between temporal continuity and the type of singularity constituted by the event have witnessed the shattering of this alliance. At the end of the twentieth century, they have split or divided themselves lengthwise into two apparently autonomous, not to say opposing branches: an inferior branch, that of communication; and a superior branch, that of the event as such. The twin ages of communication and the event have succeeded the age of his-

1. "That which is beyond being." –Tr.

tory. Why twin? I maintain that the most encompassing concept of philosophy—for I allow myself the right, one that is perhaps contentious but which I will try to legitimate, to speak of philosophy *as such* [*la philosophie*]—is that of a discourse; a special or transcendental discourse insofar as it aspires to be that of the real par excellence, but one which, on account of a degree of linguistic saturation in every way anterior to the linguistic turn, is, like all discourses, doubly-articulated. These two articulations—and here I am delineating a simple schema, the invariant of what I call 'the philosophical decision'—possess the general form of transcendence as act or operation, but inflected in two modalities that are themselves both very heterogeneous and reciprocally correlated. The first articulation, generally speaking and for simplicity's sake, is that of being and entity: it finds expression at the level of the *meta* and tends to be 'ecstatico-horizonal' and ontico-ontological, to adopt two Heideggerian expressions in a simplified, descriptive sense. This articulation constitutes a historico-systematic structural a priori proper to the philosophies of communication that are developing globally within the domains of the *meta* and the universal project, albeit not without brushing up against the event both in its inferior, general or representational aspect, that of the media for instance, and in its superior aspect, which Heidegger, for example, upholds as *Ereignis*. The second articulation tends to be that of being and the One. It is no longer spoken of in terms of the *meta* but of the *epekeina*: it has an 'ecstatico-vertical' form and ultimately has the real as One rather than as being for its object—albeit the One only insofar as it is simultaneously Other. It constitutes a historico-systematic structural a priori proper to those philosophies of the event that are developing globally within the dimension of the *epekeina*.

Thus the event corresponds to another articulation, one that is emergent relative to the transcendence of being. It constitutes a rupture within being, history, time, only by exceeding horizontal depth as well as the merely horizontal interval, thereby constituting an emergence at the same time as a rupture, but a rupture in excess of horizontal transcendence. It is the One-as-Other and sometimes, but then more Judaically, the Other-as-One. It goes without saying that there is no empirical event—it would be dissolved in the indifference of generality and particularity. On the other hand, the event may sometimes provide the basis for a superior empiricism. Whatever the case, the event is not merely the result of superimposing an ontology onto a history, but rather it introduces a new order. It does not even merge with being, whether being be construed as presence, or as pure multiplicity without presence, or as regularity once more. It appears whenever there is a repression, a cutting, or a collapsing of being. The event thereby indexes a more general ground which may be, depending on the case, an order of presence, of effects or singularities rather than of generalities, of multiplicities or of the multiple rather than of unity. It indexes an ontological ground with which it remains complicit even as it detaches itself from it. This ontological ground, generated by the *meta,* can disappear or fade; it may occasionally become forbidden, repressed, or subjected to various operations. Generally speaking, it is the composite forms of this ground that are eliminated: the composite of the One and the multiple, for example; and in this case the event depends solely on a being that is radically multiple and inconsistent. Or, in another instance, the composite of being and particular entity is eliminated: in this case the event remains dependent upon a universal Being-One devoid of particularity.

Thus, from our point of view Deleuze gives a standard, philosophically average description of the event because he brings together all its transcendental conditions in perfect equilibrium. The event connects a base of pure, ideal, infinite continuity, an a priori but non-empirical regularity, a curve that carries it; and a rupture or emergence that is at least unilateral and irreversible. Nietzsche and Deleuze empty Platonism of its intermediary composites and identify the extremes. They fold the *epekeina* back onto the *meta* without erasing the former. In doing so they assemble an 'over-position,' a logic of the 'over,' of overcoming and overview. The event is geostationary, so to speak: it oversees and carries off history and the world as an eternal One that is coextensive with the multiple. The event is over-cut, line of flight, tendential limit [*limite tendancielle*], relative-absolute cut rather than interruption.

Derrida on the contrary maintains the duality, the heterogeneity of the two forms of transcendence, as well as the rootedness of the *epekeina* within the *meta*. He maintains the former's excess of transcendence over the latter but at the same time bends it back toward itself and accentuates in the event that aspect of it which constitutes an 'inhibition' or 'interruption' of the logos or presence. Generally speaking, the two forms of transcendence are bound together through co-belonging—this is an invariant—and can only be separated through abstraction. In other words, one trails the other at its base or periphery, partially containing it according to a relation of domination that differs in each case.

Communication and event divide between themselves philosophy's unique destiny. Even if these two forms of transcendence find themselves competing with one another in separate philosophies, they are always combined according to varying relations and proportions. These combinations contain the One, the Other, Being, and the particular entity as transcendental components of the event. Their combinations amount to so many transcendental equations of the event; equations mapping and developing philosophy's space of possibilities within the ambit of its most encompassing concept. Although one can distend the event through any one of its dimensions or aspects, it is always possible to pin it to the four corners of the philosophical decision and to inscribe it within the space of the latter. Such is the span and stature of the event, its non-punctuality, its internal complexity.

We can generalize deconstruction, so to speak: the event is not the other of the logos but the other of/in philosophy defined according to the wider aspect of its complex structure, rather than exclusively in terms of 'presence.' The event occurs at the margins of philosophy, only at its margins; but by inserting the total invariant of philosophy within it, we modify its concept: philosophy's calculation of the event, the event's philosophically calculable character, is its least well-known aspect, but this aspect alone is what allows its character as incalculable, or as One-Other, to 'exist.'

Thus, the widened concept of the event is coextensive with that of philosophy and hence with the world, and puts into play the totality of the great transcendentals. Each philosophy now cuts or carves out 'its' event from this crystal by valorizing or suspending the One or the Multiple, the One or Being, Being or the particular entity. This labor of remarking or subtraction, of accentuation or cutting, answers to a few invariants: the invariance of its transcendental structures regardless of the empirical knowledge that effectuates them; the invariance of the event's position as succeeding ontology or onto-theology, in an apparently derivative, but in actuality ultimate and therefore originary position; finally, the invariance of the event affected by the suspension of the inferior or superficial forms of representation, particularly those composite forms in which the transcendentals are combined. The event is a constantly simplified combination of these transcendentals, one shorn of intermediate forms. But all these operations presuppose the totality of philosophical operations, with the event appearing at the limits of this totality through a series of gestures designed to allow the dimension of the *epekeina* to manifest itself.

Philosophy posits the event as a real in itself, but in reality it is the effect of a philosophical decision, inscribed within the order of possibilities proffered by philosophy, with regard to which it constitutes the most extreme form as well as the highest realization. If the event focuses within its apparently ineffable simplicity the entire structure of what I call the philosophical decision, along with its double-articulation, then inversely this decision is itself the proto-event, the self-positing of the event, and hence the event which contains its own reason: 'the philosophy or world-event.' It then becomes necessary to maintain both that the philosophies of the event, insofar as they are manifold and opposing philosophies, particular combinations of the *meta* and the *epekeina*, are not 'events,' since there is nothing older than the philosophy that encompasses them; *and* that philosophy, which is not particular, is the only event or the essence, the 'eventality' of the event, since there is nothing more emergent, more exceptional and singular than philosophy. Corollary: the philosophies of the event remain affiliated, directly in some cases, indirectly in others, with the far-from-novel attempt, intrinsic to every philosophy, but particularly accentuated and re-marked since Nietzsche and Heidegger, to enclose philosophy within itself, to raise it up to the apex of its emerging juncture, to make philosophy gather and transcend itself in its entirety as *epekeina* both towards itself and towards the real as One or One-Other. If the event illuminates and nourishes history, the world, and existence, this is precisely because it is this lightning, this originary flash of which the Platonic sun is merely the effect or residue in the human eye—an effect of the sun or a luminous spot.

How Identity Is at Stake in the Event: Transition to Non-Philosophy

We have set out the problem of attaining a rigorous thought of the event. We have universalized what the event exceeded, the logos, in the form of philosophy itself, now distilled down to the structure of the One-Other, and we have thereby universalized the event in the form of philosophy as such. But now the problem takes on an altogether different form: what would be the structure of an event capable of exceeding philosophy or the One-Other itself; that is to say, of exceeding the world in the expanded sense we have given to this term, without remaining reciprocally bound to it in any way? This is the problem of non-philosophy.

Identity and event: these terms seem to evoke a play of metaphysical entities. But what is at issue here is the possibility of a thinking of the event that would be at once more rigorous and less circular than that of philosophy; the possibility of a theory that would prize the event free from the realm of the philosophies of history; a theory that would no longer construe the event as the mere crest of time's wave or as the excess of philosophy or the world over themselves; even if this also requires thinking the event in terms of a certain relation to this commonly accepted and undeniable conception.

On the face of it there would seem to be nothing more irreconcilable than identity and event. Yet identity is implicated in the event, and, I would like to suggest, implicated in a variety of heterogeneous ways. Following the suggestions proposed above, I shall define 'philosophy,' notwithstanding all the slight variations in the 'philosophies of the event,' in terms of the convertibility of identity and event; a convertibility that is only assured so long as philosophy is not fetishistically reduced to its objects or its entities, but grasped in the totality of its operations. Conversely, I shall define what I call 'non-philosophy' in terms of the non-convertibility, or of a duality that I call 'unilateral,' of identity and event.

If philosophy, whatever its posture, defines the event in terms of identity plus a few other determinations, then it reciprocally makes of identity as such an event, albeit one that is probably exceptional or extreme. Non-philosophy, on the other hand, refuses this convertibility; it does not turn identity into an event but determines the event unilaterally through identity as real presupposition of thought. Accordingly, this thesis is not without relation to philosophy—it has a philosophical 'ring' or 'resonance,' it bears a well known air of 'family resemblance' to it—and yet for all that it is not properly speaking 'philosophical' in the sense which I have begun to give to this word. Identity thus has a double status: as actively involved in philosophy, mixed with alterity or difference and ascribed higher functions of synthesis or consistency; but also, and in sharp contrast, as real presupposition of thought, as a real that I shall characterize as being without essence, without donation, without consistency or form—for identity 'in flesh and blood' is in fact none of these things, even when, as above, it passes for that which provides consistency and form. Let us first quickly examine its status within philosophy.

According to philosophy, the event is already essentially related to identity, and not merely related to it as that which it seeks to destroy or overcome, but essentially related to it in its transcendental form as One-Other, rather than in its ontico-ontological form. However, this aspect is generally understood in a truncated manner, or the event interpreted through that which it overcomes. This is an appearance of representational and metaphysical origin. The event is perceived as if it were without identity, and even as that which dissolves identity. Identity in the event is initially understood in term of inferior forms, as ontic and/or ontological, but not as beyond these, for the One-Other is as much alterity as identity. It is not surprising then that the event cuts into, represses, or overcomes these representational forms of identity and that the problem of the identity of the event has become incomprehensible and paradoxical, or cynically and dogmatically understood as the quasi-material identity of the event as 'thing.' Because identity is already understood as belonging to objects in themselves, and since the event apparently does not refer back to itself, the latter is from the very outset drawn toward the multiplicity and singularity harbored within a merely apparent unity. Consequently, there results the idea that the event presupposes an indefinite multiplicity of individually unassignable causes and that it requires a hermeneutics to decipher its multiple possible meanings.

Against these metaphysical appearances, it is in any case necessary to re-establish identity within the event. But the real problem still lies elsewhere: the event does not lack identity, but is identity's desire for itself. Its aspect as Other and its aspect as One are adjoined without distance. The event is a decision of identity, an identification, and furthermore it solicits a corresponding decision: one must will it or accept it, cause it to occur or undergo it, desire it, affirm it or over-affirm it. When all is said and done, the event thinks itself just as philosophy *as such* [*la philosophie*] thinks itself: thus it is only apparently a non-decision. It has a decision as its inverse; it is an undecidable decision.

Understood in this way, in accordance with all its dimensions, the event is not only affiliated to multiplicity but also to identity. And it is not only affiliated to the in-itself but just as equally to desire. It is even the identification of identity and desire. The event matters to philosophy as the real that finally appears at the limits of its ideal abstractions. It marks the apex of its effort and its will. Philosophy is desire of the real and hence desire of the event. The event is its own awaiting, it is accompanied by prayer and petition, or by desire, and this desire is part of its complete constitution. It is a desired identity, rather than an identity 'in-person.' It is a locus of reversal, a revolutionary pivot, a point of transvaluation, an inaugural rupture, a turning in thought, an appeal that takes aback or interpellates…It is an object of desire and sometimes of Messianic awaiting…It is for the same reason that philosophy is an event, or is in the final analysis a thinking of the All as event, and that it is not a theory of the event. The event even seems to be the non-theorizable par excellence, an absolute limit for the theoretical grasp, requiring other modes of approach: a non-objective thought, a turning in thought, a willing of the event or an affect of its reception, etc.

All of this, which is still philosophical, announces the non-philosophical perspective, but announces it as wholly other. What would a non-philosophical event be? An event that is not structured or determined in its essence by philosophy and capable of taking the philosophy-event as its object? Obviously, it would itself be the theory of this philosophy-event. But it then becomes evident that this theory-event merely has a philosophical aspect, one not positing or determining itself, but determined instead by the real, the One, or identity insofar as these are given rather than insofar as they are desired. In other words, the event will remain primary but will no longer itself be the real to which philosophy aspires. In order to defeat idealism, that of philosophy as such rather than the merely restricted version of it found in the famed 'idealist positing,' a real presupposition for thought is necessary, and this presupposition must be a real given totally, unconditionally, and without any act of giving; a given that is not the result of a givenness. In philosophy this real is the One, but philosophy identifies it with Being, with ideality and transcendence: it is the hybrid of the One-Other. The non-philosophical transformation then consists in modifying the axioms of thought at a global level according to a new experience of the real as without-being and without-otherness, a real which I shall characterize as non-consistent, devoid of ontological consistency, and simply as in-One.

We shall consequently distinguish all of the ideal structures of philosophy, or even its composite structures, which are part-ideal, part-real, from the real defined in terms of the non-consistency of a One which is no longer the apex of philosophy. Philosophy continuously ups the ante in the search for the event's ideal conditions of possibility until it finally attains its real condition, the One-Other. But the *epekeina* aims at a real that is transcendent and does so in a manner that is still ecstatic. Non-philosophy does not invert the vector of philosophy, transcendence, but substitutes the real, the real presupposition, which is to say radical immanence, for the event's transcendent construction as part-ideal, part-real. The real presupposition is identity as such, that which is not predicated of the entity, of Being, of the Other, or even of itself: an identity of immanence, one which is non-consistent. The radical One does not consist within itself.

This non-consistent given, which can alone determine a thinking *for* philosophy but not philosophy itself, is not obtained as a result of some form of scientific cognition taking over from philosophical ontology. The real cannot be given according to a scientific mode of cognition or one which would be at once scientific and ontological, by means of an operation of scission within philosophy, an operation rejecting the

One and philosophical ontology. It cannot be given through a mathematical donation at once external to philosophy yet also sufficiently internal to be capable of arrogating its ontological function, thereby effecting a decisive resolution 'within' the concept of philosophy as a whole. This refusal immediately puts into play the conception one has of the event. The latter is ordinarily conceived as being without reason, without a why, without an assignable cause. The mode of the event we are describing, the thinking of the philosophy-event, is certainly without a why, an origin, or an end, but it is more generally without reason, and this absence of an external reason does not amount to a self-causing or *causa sui* of the event. On the contrary, this event constituted by the thinking that is of and for philosophy is determined by a cause but only in-the-last-instance, a feature which maintains its relative autonomy. It cannot be a cause in one of the four metaphysical senses (formal, final, efficient, material). The real is nothing ontic, nor ontological, nor even heterological—it is an instance of manifestation of the world of philosophy—but a 'last instance,' or a power of manifestation-in-the-last-instance. Correlatively, it is the One-in-One that is the real content of the supposed identification of the scientific-mathematical and the ontological, and which constitutes the real or last instance of presupposition for this identification. The distinction, which is crucial for us here, between the real-according-to-philosophy (the philosophically consistent real of the One-Other), and the non-consistent real, is extended into the distinction between philosophy and theory as identity-in-the-last-instance of science and philosophy:

1. A theory of the event must apply to 'philosophy' itself as invariant event of every philosophy of the event; its object is the convertibility of 'philosophy' and event—the world or philosophy-event—rather than this or that local event within the

supposed horizon of philosophy. The world-event is effectively the set of the philosophies of the event (of its transcendental equations): there is no pure event or event-in-itself, except as a philosophical appearance.

2. A theory of the world-event (we will abbreviate the latter as 'event') cannot itself be just a philosophy or just a science, it must be a certain combination of the two, one determined-in-the-last-instance. It must possess a scientific aspect so as not to duplicate its object in a sterile fashion, and a philosophical aspect so as not to remain foreign to philosophy and to be capable of relating to the latter without denying or dismembering it. We shall call unified theory of the event the theory that elaborates itself as identity of science and philosophy.

3. The identity of science and philosophy is not their epistemological or more generally their philosophical co-belonging. This would be a contradictory conception and one doomed to failure. In light of the preceding conditions, this identity is altogether special. On the one hand, it is not a scientific object, such as a type of knowledge; but neither, on the other hand, is it a philosophical object, such as the One-Other, for example. We shall say that it is an identity only in-the-last-instance of science and philosophy. The problem which then arises concerns the nature of this presupposition and its relation to thought. Moreover, if it identifies science and philosophy with a view to determining the theory of the event, it does so only through their minimal invariant, their 'posture,' rather than in terms of particular modes of knowledge, theories, or doctrines. Theory is theoretical insofar as it is able to produce a non-specular cognition concerning the event-object, and it is philosophical, which is to say basically transcendental, insofar as it constitutes itself with and for this object to which it relates itself in a relation that is transcendental rather than one of objective cognition. 'Non-philosophy' is at its starting

point a 'transcendental science' in a sense which is no longer Husserlian or philosophical, but rather that of an identity-in-the-last-instance of science and philosophy.

4. The ultimate problem is no longer that of the 'cause of the event.' On the one hand, the cause is here cause of the theory of the event, short of lapsing into cynicism or materialism. On the other, it is cause of the theory of the world-event, not of this or that event as conceived by this or that philosophy, even as it fails to scrutinize the totality of operations required for carving it out. We shall summarize all these clarifications by saying that the sought-after cause determines-in-the-last-instance the unified theory of the world-event.

Lastly, we distinguish three modes of the event: (1) the intra-philosophical event or event-object of philosophies; (2) the world-event with its philosophical form, or philosophy as such, insofar as it constitutes the prototypical or originary event; (3) the rigorous theory (that of the world-event) as non-philosophical advent [*Avènement*]; one which is still primary but dependent on a cause of-the-last-instance.

From the Philosophy-Event to the Non-Philosophical Advent

Let us attempt to construct the theoretical apparatus that draws all these conditions together. I am putting it forward here without providing its detailed analysis. With this goal in mind, can we identify an exemplary existing form of cognition, with a view to transforming it so as to furnish it with an essential philosophical sense, that is to say, a transcendental pertinence? Can we identify, according to the general non-philosophical conditions of the One or real, a structure of thought incorporating the donation of the philosophy-event as object at once universal in form and contingent and variable in content? In other words, the non-philosophical event we seek under the name of the advent should, in conforming to this structure, distinguish itself from its object while relating to it in the manner of a kind of knowing [*savoir*], but also relate to it transcendentally in the manner of a philosophy. This cognitive matrix is probably, give or take its non-philosophical transformation, the form of the function, albeit not exactly that of the function in its mathematical usage, since it must now also receive an intrinsically transcendental use. We thereby propose substituting the 'function' form, while modifying it in a sense that we will progressively specify, for philosophical syntaxes such as those of the dialectic, difference, the order of reasons, etc.

The role of the constant is obviously assumed by the instance of the One-in-One, which is not just any constant but the constant par excellence, identity personified, that which universalizes the new apparatus and renders it immanent. The One as constant is by definition the condition required for the production of a non-specular cognition, one which is heterogeneous to its object, the One being radically foreclosed to philosophy and to the latter's specific causality. But since it is at the same time able to 'give' or 'manifest' philosophy in its (relative) autonomy, the real can fulfill the function of a transcendental (non-arithmetical) constant.

The role of argument or variable is taken by the world-event, which is an invariant structure, but one that is always clothed and given through particular variations. What is important is that any philosophical content whatsoever, provided it has the invariant form of what we call the philosophical decision, can fulfill the condition of the variable. In this instance it is the theme or content known as 'event,' but it is now the supreme exemplar of the event, the one constituted by philosophy and given through distinct realizations. Thus, as given-in-One or manifested by the One, the advent will be a transcendental function of the philosophy-event, which is to say, in this context, and in accordance with these new, obviously non-Kantian conditions, a transcendental function which is real-in-the-last-instance.

What do we mean by a 'transcendental function' if the former term is no longer to be understood in its Kantian sense? The real or One is given without an operation of givenness, manifested without an operation of manifestation. It is not split in two, divided and represented by itself, posited by itself, cause of itself, or passive effect of itself. This suffices to ensure its universality, that is to say, to ensure that it allows philosophy itself to be also given, and to give it according to its own modality which is that of the 'without-givenness.' There is a givenness of philosophy, but it is a self-givenness which has no effect on that being-given which the real as such is. The real, on the other hand, gives philosophy's self-givenness according to its own modality of being-given. Yet, insofar as the real gives nothing, and particularly not philosophy, but rather brings its own being-given (without-givenness) to the latter, or better still (since philosophy is in any case given according to its own modality) insofar as the real gives philosophy according to the modality of this being-given (without-givenness), then the real immediately fulfills a transcendental function with regard to philosophy as such. The real is initially in itself a condition *sine qua non*, one that is negative and necessary but not sufficient. But when the variable, as we shall say, 'effectuates' the real or One, then the latter enters, without alienating itself, without losing its character as real, into a transcendental function through which it relates to philosophy, or, more precisely, through which it gives philosophy as given-in-One. We will say that it gives it or determines it only in-the-last-instance.

The non-philosophical event will then alter in its phenomenal but not in its material status with regard to the philosophical event. It shifts from the terrain of transcendence in general, and from the alterity of the *epekeina* in particular, to that of immanence. It is neither given horizontally through a phenomenological depth or distance, nor vertically through an infinity of separation. The One does not cause it to appear, like an object or mode of the subject, one side lined with invisibility and hence bilateral, or like a presence that always remains bilateral. It is not the result of a distance of objectivation, or that of a distance of alterity; on the contrary, it is a radical immanence that causes the world to spring forth otherwise. The advent is no longer in excess of the world as given, because such an excess now belongs to the world. But it also stops cancelling itself, erasing itself in itself, in the manner of a world continuously expanding and retracting. The event is in turn raised up or manifested in the form of the advent. How can we describe the latter phenomenally?

The advent, we now know, does not lie at the world's horizon and is not the other side of that horizon (Heidegger). But neither can it be said to constitute an infinity of reverse verticality, a reverse transcendence that would pierce or puncture the horizon (Levinas). The advent comes neither from afar nor from on high. It emerges as a radical solitude that it is impossible to manipulate, dominate, or reduce, like the solitude of great works of art…It no longer announces anything; it is neither absence nor presence nor even an 'other presence,' but rather unique solitude given-in-One in-the-last-instance. It emerges as the identity of a unique face without a 'face-to-face.' The world is 'facing,' it is in a state of 'facing,' in the same way in which something is said to be 'living.' This is its 'unifaciality.' The 'more' the immanence constituting the real is radical, the more the world appears outside itself or given as unique face of the world: this is its unilaterality. Unilaterality and unifaciality are not instances of the alterity belonging to the enlarged concept of event. The solitude of the unique 'facing' transforms alterity itself, since the real is even more 'other' and stranger than the Other: its 'being-other' differs because it is radical immanence. The world as given-in-One or according to the One is thereby a stranger to itself in a more radical fashion than if it were merely other-than-itself. This is precisely its solitude as 'the unique.'

On this account, the advent is delivered from every direct onto-theological determination, these determinations never going beyond the order of the variable. The advent is not more absolute than the philosophy-event, which is already absolute, but it is radical. It is not more 'originary' in some vague manner; it is archi-originary or radically first, that is to say, uni-originary, or determined-in-the-last-instance by the real as One. It is devoid in its essence of every primary content, whether ontic or ontological, historic or historical [*historial*], these remaining confined to the order of the variable. It is the event as such of rigorous transcendental thought, of theory as identity-in-the-last-instance of the scientific and the philosophical. Consequently, it is not an 'event of thought' but the advent of thought as such [*la pensée*] in its identity, that is to say, of the 'force (of) thought,' even if there is thought and knowledge before it, but in a separated state, either philosophical or scientific.

Accordingly, just as we proceeded from the event within philosophy to philosophy as prototype of the event, we have now proceeded from this prototype to an archetype which is a 'henotype' in-the-last-instance. However, understood in this way, the advent as theory or thinking for 'philosophy' as such is no longer an extension of the latter, a meta-event or over-event. Philosophy is already the event of the *meta* and, more than this, the over-event of the *epekeina*. But the advent is no longer a supplement of transcendence, of height, or of distance. It is, on the contrary, the being-given-in-One in-the-last-instance of the event; it is *for* the event; it is advent.

The advent maintains or at least recalls certain essential features of the vulgar or even philosophical conception of the event, but it transforms them:

1. Its unity? It is not so much unity as identity, not so much singularity as solitude. The One is no longer its attribute, its ultimate essence, but that which determines it, the immanent cause of the advent, rather than the transcendent cause of the event. Identity does not manifest itself in the lightning flash of the event, it is that which manifests or brings forth the advent to the world. But it achieves this at the cost of its solitude, the solitude of identity.

2. Its causality? But it is not so much transcendence outside the world or at the limits of the world, of history for instance, as it is the immanent causality of thought for the world and for history. The advent is the manner in which the philosophy-event presents itself when it is determined-in-the-last-instance by the solitude of the One. If the event constitutes a flight beyond the world, or a line of flight at best, the advent is a way of making the world and its philosophical form come forth [*advenir*] to the One or the real. There where the real is, the world in its form as philosophy must come to be [*advenir*] according to the modality of the advent.

3. To be the effect of an immanent cause, or more precisely, one acting in and through immanence, is to be in a manner of speaking without a direct cause, or at least without an assignable cause according to representation or the world. The advent is radically alien to the world on account of its cause, which is only of-the-last-instance; and relatively alien to the world on account of the material that it draws from the latter. It is bound by the world; but only in the sense of drawing its materials and its occasions from it, rather than in the

sense of requiring a foothold within it. At the same time it comes from elsewhere, rather than from the world. The real of-the-last-instance is u-topic and the advent is u-topic and u-chronic through this latter. This is its radical irreversibility, but one that is identical to its determination-in-the-last-instance.

By way of conclusion, there follow a few remarks concerning the style of what I call 'non-philosophy.' What I have just presented has all the characteristics of an abstract, second-degree theoretical construction. But (1) I lay claim to the abstract—the real or One—rather than to abstraction. The One is abstract-without-an-operation-of-abstraction; abstraction follows after and is imposed upon thought, as its form, by the real. (2) I lay claim to theory, but I understand it in terms of the radical identity of science and philosophy, which is to say, the radical identity of the two aspects: knowledge on one hand, and a transcendental usage or pragmatics of philosophy on the other. It is thus a transcendental theory or science, one providing a non-empirical, identical or 'unified' knowledge and pragmatics of the philosophy-object as form of the world. (3) Lastly, it is a theory without a primacy of the theoretical. It is, on the contrary, anti-idealist and anti-theoreticist because it is subordinated to the primacy of a real which, in this context, is not of the order of cognition, nor even of thought, consciousness, etc. This theory's determination-in-the-last-instance by the real does not indicate the philosophical position known as 'realism.' This type of real excludes realism. In virtue of its nature as a radical identity, it is more of the order of a kind of performative, or more exactly, a performed-without-performance. Non-philosophy is a theory, but one which is practical-in-the-last-instance or determined by such a practice.

Chapter 7

The Decline of Materialism in the Name of Matter

Translated by Ray Brassier

Perhaps the categories of 'idealism' and 'materialism' are doomed. But in what name? And if on the basis of an efficacy superior to that of a name, which? By virtue of which supplement? That of the idea? That of matter?

Instead of condemning them with a religious gesture, let us recall them but merely as examples of archaic, quasi-religious belief; let us treat them as instances of the old faith with a view to establishing the extent to which they are still derivative interpretations of that real = X which we seek.

Neither their distinction nor their contents are defined once and for all, but filled out and varied as doctrine dictates. Nevertheless, their use becomes strictly philosophical and autonomous relative to those sciences and politics with which they maintain relations yet to be determined once they become considered as immanent or transcendental criteria for philosophical doctrines and one of them, materialism, becomes raised to the power of index of itself and of the other, thereby becoming the bearer of their difference, which is still

This text is an extract from Laruelle's book *Le principe de minorité* [*The Minority Principle*](Paris: Aubier, 1981). The extract first appeared in English translation in *Pli: The Warwick Journal of Philosophy* 12 (2001), 33-40. The English text also appeared on the ONPhi website (www.ONPhi.net) in June, 2003.

to say, at this stage, their relation. We are treating them here as genetic a prioris, materialism relative to idealism, and both of them together relative to the contents of doctrine. We do not yet know what a 'genetic a priori' is, but if it is to remain real-and-nothing-but and otherwise-than-synthetic we will not be looking either to Kant or to Husserl for its concept. One determines materialism's genetic difference from idealism, at the same time as one determines a real, otherwise-than-materialist conception of their a priori difference and its power of genesis. Against the empiricist mistake that consists in imbuing these categories with an 'immediate' content that is in reality already mediated, it is a question of conceiving of them at once in-themselves and in terms of that which is more important than they are, their relation, as well as something more important even than their relation: their absolute difference. How are we to isolate the latter? In any case, here idealism and materialism no longer refer back to:

1. Supposedly given objects (Matter and the Idea in the state of quality and quantity, techno-economic production and ideology). To talk of matter, to designate either it or the sciences of matter, is not sufficient in order to produce a genuinely materialist assertion, or even—which would only be one of its traits among others—an immanent one. The problem here is no longer that of a 'materialist' discourse or knowledge of matter, but of an enunciation that would itself be intrinsically material—which, as anyone will admit, is not bound to turn that enunciation into a thing just because one would no longer make of it a discourse about a thing.

2. Conceptual significations, 'idealism' and 'materialism' as conceptual generalities. Such generalities always contain a reference to qualities given in experience. They are mixtures, combining general traits of matter, but ones taken from the sciences of nature, with more empirical traits taken from the

perception of nature. These significations constitute variables that always suppose an immediate or empirical notion of the real and matter in the name of the particular value that exemplifies them. They are the staple of pre-structural Marxism.

3. Meanings that are supposedly produced rather than expressed. In 'structural' Marxism, 'idealism' and 'materialism' become categories devoid of conceptual signification yet still endowed with a differential meaning produced through the interplay of theoretical and political positions, and principally characterized by their differential relation, their combination and determination *relative* to one another. If the line of demarcation we seek no longer passes between objects (Matter/Idea), or concepts, or even enunciateds, are the immanent criteria not concealed within the materialist or idealist *modality*? By modality we do not mean, as Kant did, knowledge's relation to the subject and to the three types of condition of possibility (formal, real, necessary), but rather meaning's or the enunciated's *relation* to differential elements that are themselves devoid of meaning while conditioning it. Difference then becomes conceived as a power of non-sense within sense, as a genetic power of sense. But the new problem, the limit of this attempt, becomes: what is a *relative* non-sense or difference worth? Considered as differential, genetic or problematic elements conditioning the contents of doctrine, 'idealism' and 'materialism' no longer refer back to an intuitive figure of the Idea or of Matter, or to a concept or essence, nor even to an ideological phantasm or fiction. But the risk lies in confusing what we must seek, the essence of 'materialism' and 'idealism' as differential, a priori, material elements, with the *structuralist* version of this essence, which is relative and hence necessarily ideal. Doubtless, we no longer invest this essence with the empirical properties of things, concepts or pure forms, but we will be reintroducing ideality into it if we

continue to say, as structuralism does, that 'materialism' and 'idealism' are differential positions that are *relative* to one another, or if we continue to conflate—along with structuralism, Nietzsche, and idealism in general—difference with a *relation of reciprocal determination* between two positions. These a priori differential elements are characterized neither by a sensible figure, nor a conceptual element, nor even a phantasmatic or imaginary irreality. *But neither can they be characterized by a supra-conceptual form of ideality, by an ideal nature comprising relation or relativity.*

As far as such categories are concerned, one distinguishes between their sense or content as categories on the one hand—these are genuinely relations, and there is from this point of view a modality proper to enunciateds as enunciateds—and their differential elements or their enunciation on the other hand. But this is precisely where the problem lies: are these elements themselves *relative*, in the manner in which, for instance, reciprocally relative *positions* are, mutually determining each other in a continuous tendency or becoming—becoming-materialist, becoming-idealist, becoming-revolutionary? Is their scission still a secondary form, a variant, of their unity? A synthesis of opposites reflecting itself into itself? The essence of materialism lies, as we have seen, in *hyletism*, in the (structural) positing or (Nietzschean) affirmation of the continuous, synthetic and consequently ideal essence proper to these differential a prioris. One gets an inkling here of the enormous philosophical quid pro quo nourishing structuralism, as well as the super-structural thinking engendered by Nietzsche and Heidegger, and which is that of the systems of Difference: the most immediate (intuitive and conceptual) forms of unity and ideality are expunged, but neither structuralism nor Nietzscheism, and the former far less than the latter, are able to see that unity and ideality are still conserved by them in the superior form of a pure continuity, of the Same. The signifier is in no way a heterogeneous sensible matter, it is just as much a continuity and an ideality, the inscription of a very relative heterogeneity within a form or a presence (the signifier *represents* the subject for another signifier), a materiality rather than a matter, a synthesis effected as the result of relativity and one that constitutes the differential elements themselves. Similarly, the *hyle* proper to 'the will to power' subsumes the real under relations of force that remain ideal and continuous even in their 'difference.'

We have been deluding ourselves: as far as the processes of 'structure' (signifying entities as ideal and thus continuous) and of 'machines' (forces and powers as a-signifying entities, but ideal and continuous nevertheless) are concerned, there can only ever be a relative materialist 'overturning' of idealism. In the primacy of 'relations' (of production, of forces, of texts, of power) which we took to be materialism and which indeed is one in effect, that is to say, a rejection of idealism, there is only ever a *transfer* of difference in and as the idea, a generalized *meta-phor* of multiplicity folded back onto the continuous, a radical modalization of thought, an ultimate primacy of ideality over the real, of being over the entity.

At this point, we find ourselves teetering on the cutting-edge of contemporary philosophy, perched on the edge of an abyss wherein everything could be lost once more. How can we not make of absolute or dispersive difference—which is only a program for the time being—an ideal or relative entity in the manner not only of the different variants of structuralism, but also of Nietzsche, Heidegger, and deconstruction? How can we attain *a concept of difference that would be real and genetic as well as a priori and transcendental* without re-inscribing it once more, if not within the sphere of signification, at least within that of ideal sense, in the pure *typos* and *topos* of the idea? In becoming relative to one another, the terms of difference lose their absolute or independent character as empirical entities, but only in order to cede this 'bad' absoluteness to their relation, which only ceases being relative to its terms by becoming relative to itself. 'Materialism' and 'idealism' are then no longer only two positions relative to one another, they form a complex or chiasmus, each alternately functioning as cut and as continuum, as support and as relation, for the other. It is this chiasmus, which the *hyle* supports, that constitutes 'real' materialism, as if the 'materialist' side or face of the assemblage, functioning as a continuous point of dispersion for materialism and idealism, *simultaneously* inhibited or limited the idealist side or face, and reconnected or reconstituted a continuous system, an assemblage that is necessarily idealist precisely insofar as it is an assemblage. It is idealist to the second power, to the *n*th power. In the systems of Difference in general, materialism is only idealism raised to the *n*th power, to the '*and*th' power, infinitely intensified. By elevating, in viciously circular fashion, ideality to the stage where it becomes auto-productive, which is to say *causa sui* ('the will to power'), these systems use ideality to confirm itself, thereby rendering the *genesis* of ideality and its forms impossible. From this point of view, Nietzsche, Heidegger and all the systems of Difference remain incapable of founding a genuinely immanent materialism, a becoming-'material' of thought that would no longer be a becoming-continuous, or a difference that would be a multiplicity beyond the continuous as such. They do not sufficiently reduce ideality in the definition of the differential genetic elements (which Nietzsche, for his part, called 'active forces' and 'will to power').

In other words, what we have here is merely the superior form of the old materialisms. In the last instance, it continues to subordinate matter to the ultimate possible form of the logos (the logos or idea of Matter as such), rather than subordinating the logos of Matter to matter, thereby engaging a genuinely dispersive becoming-real of ideality instead of a continuous becoming-ideal of the real. Thus, in order to remain faithful to its original inspiration and secure a definitive victory over idealism, materialism should first consent to partially eliminate itself as category and enunciated—to subordinate its materialist enunciateds to a process of enunciation that would be material, relative, or *hyletic* in itself, then stop conceiving of this enunciation as an ideal and relative process. This would be *the decline of materialism in the name of matter, and of matter as* hyle *in the name of the real.* Neither materialism nor the amphibology, the limitless fusion of the real with ideality in the *hyle*, but a more secret knowing of matter, one that would no longer employ the luminous paths of the logos…

From the outset, along with the tradition, we posed the problem in terms that precluded any solution that would not be either viciously circular or contradictory, which is to say, in terms of the relations between idealism and materialism. With such a starting point, it becomes impossible not to render idealism and materialism relative to one another, not to synthesize them in a continuous and ideal becoming-materialist, not to subordinate matter once more to its logos, not to remain frenetically idealist in one's materialism. Perhaps we should proceed otherwise and place the totality of relations, of their relations, on one side, that of ideality, and formulate the central thesis we wish to oppose to Marxism as well as Nietzscheism thus: *idealism and materialism are reciprocally relative, and both are relative to or identical with the real—while the real is not relative to them, or distinguishes itself absolutely from them.*

Such 'relations' (of causality, of unilateral or reciprocal determination) exist, but, such is the paradox of this thesis, whatever their variable content, even as 'reciprocal' they belong in the last instance only to the idealist formulation of the problem, they are the only means idealism (and materialism as formulation of the logos of Matter) has of formulating and resolving this problem. But on the other hand, materialism—or preferably matter, for this would not be true of the category of Matter—or, even more preferably, the real (matter before the *hyle*)—does not enter into relation with idealism and materialism. In the enunciated, such relations remain dominant, appropriating materialism's 'difference' from idealism, but in the enunciation, to which the enunciated must be subordinated, these relations become the secondary aspect of the assemblage. As enunciation, idealism too is also, by virtue of its real content, *without relation* to the categories or enunciateds of idealism, while as enunciated, it remains strictly relative to absolute 'material' assemblages. Moreover, this is the very basis on which idealism is in turn able to formulate all the above points in terms of objects, enunciateds, concepts, empirical entities, or, at best, in terms of relations that are either given or in the process of being produced.

As enunciated, materialism proceeds in the same fashion, issuing enunciateds, theses, imperatives and sometimes knowledges about matter or concerning matter rather than the idea, thought and their primacy. But as enunciation, materialism remains—by virtue of its own force insofar as a relation is ideality's work rather than its own—*without relation* to idealism or to the categories of matter. It cancels itself as materialism. It refuses to formulate the problem of immanent criteria in terms of the modality of the enunciated, unless it be in order to affirm the subordination of the ideal reciprocal relation between matter and ideality to the real of difference. To characterize an enunciation in terms of a modality or assemblage is still to reduce it to an enunciated, it is to sink back into idealism and its 'materialist' variants. What renders an enunciated 'material'—or rather 'real'—and not merely materialist can be demonstrated neither in terms of its objects, nor its meaning or signification, nor by its *materiality* as enunciated, that differential materiality or relatively indivisible and *continuous* distance *relating* it to other enunciateds. As far as the enunciated is concerned, at least insofar as it is grasped in its essence, to be 'materialist' is never a question of the manner in which it relates to other enunciateds, but consists rather in its refusing to enter into a relation, a becoming or mediating tendency, refusing to allow itself to be inscribed within the strategy of a reciprocity, the economy of a community, into the trade between 'positions,' 'forces,' or 'powers.'

All we have provided here are negative indications rather than a positive elaboration of 'matter' as real of the a priori genetic difference before the idea, which is to say, before the form of the a priori as such. We must simultaneously construct the 'materialist,' or rather real, concept of distinction, difference, or the discernible, and the dispersive rather than differential, relative or ideal, concept of the real, the better to uncover a multiplicity that is a priori but not ideal and an a priori that is real but dispersive. Of course, it will always be possible to interpret and criticize such an attempt as 'materialist' rather than 'material': insofar as 'materialism,' or rather 'matter,' the real before the *hyle*, remains 'indefinable,' non-negotiable at least as far as concepts and categories are concerned; it breaks away and escapes in the face of a triumphant idealism, as if communication with it became impossible or proceeded by way of breakages, shatterings, ruptures, a process of continuous metaphorization. However, this is still no more than the viewpoint of a logic or a theory. The issue is not that of a negative materiology versus a generalized metaphorics. From our point of view, such a materio-logos continues to maintain the positivity of a logos, and the apparently non-apophatic effects of a negative discourse on matter continue to inscribe themselves within this positivity. By virtue of its absolutely immediate essence, a 'matter' as pure real beyond the idea is by definition that which can never become the object of that knowledge taking the form of an ideality or horizon of being, or become the object of a negative and/or affirmative (materio)-logy whose internal constitution would be the same as the former's. The self-negation of the logos only negates certain forms of knowing: those that remain inscribed within the logos, those that remain subordinated to the concept, those placing themselves within the perspective of the idea. Just as there is a 'matter' beyond the idea and beyond the *hyle*, there is likewise—insofar as we are beyond the distinction between knowing and the real—a knowing beyond ideal essence. No rational, ratiocinative or merely logical argument will be able to overcome the resistance proper to this knowing (perhaps we should write gnosis?)—a knowing identical to those immediate data belonging to a transcendental experience (of) the One—through which we know that even the light of the idea is still relative, relative to this gnosis as to an absolute knowing. Materialism still concedes far too much to idealism, and the gnosis of 'matter,' the otherwise-than-materialist gnosis of the dispersive real, must be sought beyond materialism and beyond the *hyle*. It is a supplement for materialism as such, but a supplement of matter rather than of materialism, and a supplement of the real rather than of matter, consonant with a new interpretation of the '*veritas transcendentalis*.' Another *Kehre*? A new turning beyond the Idea's accomplished form as presence, 'will to power' and 'Eternal Recurrence,' Being? Certainly not a turning...Only the path of the Idea, of Being, of ontological ideality, knows and tolerates such turnings. We seek a multiplicity beyond essence, one that is as discontinuous, as un-Nietzschean, as possible…one that is immediately given.

Chapter 8

Determination-in-the-Last-Instance

Translated by Taylor Adkins

First Elucidation of the Determination-in-the-Last-Instance (DLI)

The determination-in-the-last-instance, invented by Marx-Engels for historical materialism, never received from them a concept adequate to the simultaneous production of all the theoretical and critical effects within its capacity. It has been understood in a far too empirical manner, assimilated to models of ontico-regional, physical and chemical causality (theory of gases, composition of forces) that are completely inadequate to the foundation of a new science of history and society, let alone the thought-world. Thus it has been fashionable to dialecticize and re-philosophize the DLI, folding it with what it should properly replace and suspend, namely the dialectic as the essence of philosophy under its most theoretical and idealist form through its materialist reversal, which is seemingly more capable of rejuvenating it (confusion of the real of immanence with matter). Marx's great discovery—of unilateral

This text is a translation of the third chapter of Laruelle's book *Introduction au non-marxisme* (Paris: PUF, 2000), 39-55. An earlier version of this translation appeared on the Speculative Heresy website (www.speculativeheresy.wordpress.com) in July, 2008.

causality against all the philosophical phantasms of reciprocity and convertibility—has remained fallow without having been exploited in its non-philosophical capacity [*puissance*], which is more heretical than philosophically 'revolutionary.' So as to elucidate the DLI in our style, i.e. make its Marxist forms seem like simple symptoms and models of a more radical concept of causality, our method follows three periods, the third being the most important for our purposes. The first period reassembles its Marxist statements and usages—these are known. The second consists in 'listening to' the first immediate quasi-phenomenological suggestions that contain the same formula as the DLI, treating them as a prioris that give the DLI, and then transforming them. The third, which we shall particularly develop, endeavors to 'ground' these a priori traits in a real-transcendental way and, better still, to determine them as belonging to the same real or to the immanent infrastructure as its most proper causality.

Following the simple formulation of the DLI allows us to posit these three traits:

1. It is a question of a causality which could be called unique, except that it calls for or supposes another, as if it were the only one yet nevertheless insufficient. Thus there are two causalities, one being primary, the other secondary, but both insufficient in their own way. Heterogeneous yet necessary to one another so as to form a unique causality, they have—or it has—this paradoxical nature of being precisely a single causality, although formed by two pieces that remain two and do not synthesize or form a system. Nevertheless, it is not a question of 'difference,' the co-extension of the One and the Two, or of the One that is Two and the Two that is One in a reversible way. The DLI instead seems to have to be irreversible, for the One is nothing but One, even with the Two, and the Two forms a Two with the One only from its point of view as Two.

2. Another trait of this syntax-without-synthesis signifies that all secondary causality, if it be multiple, is only accounted for and introduced in the final 'calculation' on the condition of 'passing' through the primary trait or through the infrastructure in regard to which the secondary cause is, by definition, 'indebted,' or which gives the secondary its new or irreducible power of causality in its re-appropriation by the thought-world, i.e. by the infrastructure's own logic. What does 'passing through' signify, or how are the One and the Two articulated?

3. The final trait that is completely phenomenologically apparent in the formula that we have taken as a symptom is the nature of the quasi-invariant or constant of the 'last instance,' in opposition to the variations of nature or region and the variability of secondary causality.

These somewhat a priori traits condition the intelligibility of the DLI, allowing it to be given through them. It now remains, from the non-Marxist perspective, to explain them on the basis of the real or the immanent concept of infrastructure; more exactly, to determine them as a syntax imposed by the infrastructure, and to make their Marxist forms seem like their restrained symptoms and models.

Misadventures of Immanence (from Spinoza to Henry)

In philosophy, including Marxism, immanence is an objective, a proclamation, an object, never a manner of thinking or a style.

The recent history of Marxism has been oriented by the following question: given that the Hegelian context does not stand any real chance, which philosophers should we turn to so as to re-activate and universalize it? To Spinoza (the parallelism of the object and knowledge, their unity without origin or end)? To the phenomenology of immanence (labor power as the ontology of the radical individual)? To Nietzsche (the trans-individual)? To Epicurus (aleatory materialism)?

Spinoza's philosophy brought about the idea of a real causality of immanence, but the Spinozist ensemble remains inscribed—at least what is recognized after Fichte—in the transcendence of a quasi-thing above consciousness or man. The philosophy of life and its auto-affection (M. Henry) reinforces immanence, albeit through a more 'absolute' than 'radical' mode, and overcomes any causality of the real by positing it in a simultaneously abstract and transcendental way, on the one hand, and as concrete labor alienated from the exterior in an incomprehensible way through commercial exchange, on the other. In order to construct non-Marxism, a real identity even more immanent than Spinoza's is necessary, a cause without-All and without-synthesis or even expression; and a causality proper to this identity rather than the mediation of an alienation by the world or capitalism. It is noteworthy that in these two cases [of Spinoza and Henry] the DLI, which is conceived of as the aid of the One-All of substance or of the One of transcendental Life, is unthinkable, insufficient, and transient. Causality always risks being lost in transcendence, as with Spinoza, even if it is called 'immanent' (this is the distinction between an 'immanent causality' and a causality *of* or *through* immanence). Or, as with Henry, it risks being lost in immanence itself as simple interiority, where it disappears and becomes transcendental, yet still coupled as labor power with the empirically-given, unintelligible mechanism of commercial exchange.

It is in the DLI as causality of the One-real rather than of Being that the two aspects of causality and the real-without-Being are unified. In the name of causality, we must stop projecting the DLI into transcendence; in the name of immanence, we must stop reducing the DLI to a merely transcendental immanence so as to then project it as pretentiously real under the form of the auto-generation of Life. The DLI is a simultaneously real, universal, immanent, and heterogeneous or critical causality, and through these characterizations, it does not return to the four forms of the causality of Being (final, material, formal, efficient). Being is not the most real, the real in-person (it is divided and supports difference); it is not the most universal (it is only a supra-generic and divided universal); nor the most immanent (it is principally defined by transcending); nor the most heterogeneous or critical (it is said of the existent and at most attains the heterogeneity of difference or, at best, the pure multiple). Perhaps no more than Hegel, Spinoza fails to fulfill these demands insofar as they are those of radicality. His single and immanent cause remains transcendent and thus alienated and alienating. The seemingly opposed interpretation of labor power as organic, individual, or monadic life (Henry), which in principle is immanent to man, still posits this life as the object of a thought for which it remains transcendent, and which also overly separates it from the critical-revolutionary aspect and 'class struggle,' from the 'world' if you will, thus condemning it to live religiously. Both philosophers [Spinoza and Henry] seemingly fulfill one of these demands but not all of them, thus actually fulfilling none.

Obliquely viewed from outside, non-Marxism can seem like a synthesis of Spinoza and Henry to even the sophisticated doctrinal Marxist. In reality, it is much more their unified theory. We shall suggest that the latter transforms the Spinozist unity of each attribute to the others into a simple *aspect* of non-Marxism, which has created the objective appearance of a transference of doctrine. Similarly, the immanence of 'individual organic life' is transformed into a simple aspect of the 'Stranger-subject' or the 'force (of) thought' as the real content of the 'proletariat.' But non-Marxism begins by reducing the efficacy of these philosophical determinations. There is no primacy of matter over consciousness, but a primacy of the real One over the matter/consciousness, being/life, and also practice/theory dyads, more globally still of the real over the thesis (of the) real, such that the former determines the latter in-the-last-instance. Here we displace Marxism and its materialism from the terrain of transcendence or capitalistic and philosophical representation onto that of radical immanence (like Henry, contrary to Spinoza), but an immanence which is real and not transcendental (like Spinoza, contrary to Henry). Only an intrinsic non-synthetic unification of these two demands in a radical perspective, in a given-without-givenness whose other name is that of 'infrastructure,' will enable us to ground these two aspects upon which these philosophers part ways and which, unified, are at the basis of non-Marxism. Thus transformed into a causality of real immanence (the DLI), these aspects make it possible to understand that Marxism's essence to come is not itself Marxist, thus reducing its varieties to a unique axiomatic.

The immanence proposed by philosophers always corresponds with models, thus to something slightly transcendent, and is never sufficiently radical to determine a thought *according to* immanence or the real-of-the-last-instance. Marxism necessarily remains the site of antinomies and draws a naïve glory from its crises and conflicts which are, even so, more philosophical than political. In any case, the individual and 'immanent life' of organic labor power (Henry) remains an immanence-entity, a transcendental-thing, precisely because it remains posited by an act of thought instead of integrally determining the latter. According to Jacobi against Fichte, materialism is vigilant against idealism but, more universally still, it must be said that the thought-world remains vigilant against the transcendental, capitalism, and labor power when these are not determined by real identity and its being-performed as the meaning of infrastructure.

This irreducibility of the real to productive forces has a precise sense: we cannot confuse labor power, individual organic life, which is still transcendent because of its theoretical status or the way in which it is posited and presupposed, with truly 'radical' and no longer absolute immanence. Such a labor power is the moment of the subject (proletariat) rather than the determining cause in-the-last-instance. Non-Marxism unilaterally (uni-laterally) distinguishes between the real, the last instance, and the subject, and thus between the 'force (of) thought' or 'practice' and 'labor power,' a distinction which ensures the inalienable nature of the real and excludes it from the incomprehensible mechanism of economic alienation through commercial exchange.

On its side, the materialist break brought about the more or less pure sense of the real against idealism but only within the interior of philosophy itself. Instead of being transcendental, it remains a simple cynicism, a primary causality between instances. Instead of subordinating the transcendental to the real, it simply remains a truncated philosophy, subtracted from itself and turned back against itself. Non-Marxism is a labor of thought and knowledge of the world—a labor of theory—and thus a transcendental thought, not a simple primary shock between instances-things. The real and the thought-world, the two extremes, *derealize* theory and the subject (the proletariat or what it remains), and oblige them to be a simple thought-knowledge. By contrast the materialist break amounts to a somewhat thing-like regionalist cynicism rather than a non-economy, non-art, etc. Materialism is not initially a non-economic thought-knowledge. The latter would be a positively non-philosophical and non-scientific thought, then applicable on the economic, political, or ethical levels through new axioms specifying its uni-versal axioms—at the risk of normalization.

Amphibologies of Materialism

The real is not, properly speaking, an 'instance' or a 'sphere' or a 'region,' to the degree that, by definition, it does not belong to the thought-world or to the world—this is the meaning of the 'last instance.' All of Marxism's objects and theoretical themes, its massively materialist (hence philosophical) economy, must therefore be reorganized and otherwise reconfigured so as to change its theoretical status. Insofar as he is also a philosopher, Marx postulates, despite certain hesitations—this is his unitary, idealist appearance—a continuity between history, its crises and mutations, and theory. This is a continuity assured by the concepts of *practice* and *contradiction* which remain philosophical (dialectical) in every way and impregnated by empiricism. Hence the amphibology of the real and the economy, under the form of the 'last instance' understood as productive forces, and which is certainly not dismantled radically when, for example, individual organic labor power is posited as the ontologico-transcendental foundation of the economy.

This confusion is in reality two-fold: between the infrastructure and a particular region (Marx's 'philosophy of the economy,' etc.), and between the diverse regions which are said to be acting directly on one another in a poorly elucidated mixture. The most dangerous confusion is that of the economy and the 'real base,' of the regional and the real. Hence an ambiguous distinction between infra- and superstructure which prohibits any explication besides a fruitless and vicious one of the thought-world as philosophy and economy, but also as philosophy and politics. The confusion of real and occasional cause compromises every interpretation of Marxism, including Marx's, be it as ontological and transcendental as we could want. Even if the following three are also appealed to, capitalistic economy and philosophy and politics, they must be intrinsically rejected as transcendent in the sphere of the thought-world to be explained; but from the perspective of the suspension of their sufficiency, they are seen as mere *aspects* within the same explanation of the thought-world. Likewise, any causality of one instance over another, if it does not pass through the mediation of philosophy-form, i.e. through the criterion of its belonging to the thought-world or the deployed concept of the superstructure, is rightly called a return to the causality of the thought-world, 'ideological' causality, and comes to prohibit a theoretical explanation of these instances or, better still, of their specifically 'reciprocal' causality. A construction between regions (economy/politics, politics/philosophy, politics/theory, economy/law, etc.) remains intra-worldly, empirical, and vicious, if it does not pass each time through a universal unified theory of each of its correlations, univocal for all, excluding any regional primacy.

Non-Marxism will therefore above all substitute, from its syntactic perspective, the unilateral duality (the 'last instance') for contradiction, 'struggle,' or 'division,' which are transcendent philosophical operators. Althusser's efforts to structurally organize the economy of these instances and escape from a 'first' and cynical materialism could only end up in a false immanence of quasi-totality (the 'All') but not of identity. The attempts to render Marxism its immanence have ended in a reinforcement of its exteriority and its transcendence. Its philosophical reconstructions generally efface, for example in a (materialist) break, a discovery that is forceful in a way different from any break. Non-Marxism is the heteronomous critique and usage—heteronomous through immanent unilaterality, not alterity—of the particular and limited nature of Marxism. Thus non-Marxism is in every way the refusal of the critique in the name of the empirical description of Marxism's failure, a failure sometimes of science, sometimes of philosophy—sometimes of one of Marxism's particular concepts which have been misunderstood or forgotten, sometimes of their philosophical or divided unity. As critique, non-Marxism manifests the reasons behind the confusion of science and philosophy, of theory and experimental reference, particularly in the themes of and insistence upon the 'real,' the 'concrete,' or 'applied Marxism.' Hence also the confusion of its objects: history and society on the one hand, productive forces and the real on the other, man and labor power, etc. These are just a few of the amphibological or generously unitary concepts furnished by the philosophical spirit that fail to ground the object of a unified theory.

Insufficiency of the Marxist DLI

Under its materialist form, the DLI possesses several general traits which should be acknowledged so as to transform and radicalize them.

1. 'Determination' is not an auto-positional act, a Kantian-critical operation of the primacy of determination over the determined. Here the reverse primacy is already announced without a return to dogmatism, albeit still under an ambiguous form. It is the determined, the real as matter-without-determination, that makes the determination. The infrastructure's nature as given does not specifically have an empirical meaning—like *Bestand* (existence)—it is instead the primacy of the given over givenness, of the determined over determination.

2. The determined-without-determination is not or is not simply the infrastructure in its empirical and regional content, but the real immanence of the latter, its power of causing or determining, such that it can be visible in the basis of labor power where it receives an organic form, but which, beyond

Marxism, must be treated as the symptom of an immanence more universal than organic, an immanence to which Marx never aspires.

3. The DLI, which is this real power of determining, is in every way an ontological and transcendental *type* of concept, even related to matter. It is not an ontic and regional concept with a physico-chemical or linguistic-structuralist model; but neither is it ontological (formal, final, efficient, and…material, which Marx forgets to exclude with the other forms of metaphysical causality). The DLI really only has meaning for the real as radical One-in-One or identity. Because of the materialist break, Marx limits it to matter, but the DLI completely implies the refusal of matter as cause (hence the efforts of certain philosophers to distinguish the category of materialism and the concept of matter…). Radical immanence can no longer take a specifying, restrictive, and transcendent ontological form like the one matter still has. It is de facto inalienable, unequal to its most distant effects—this is the 'last instance,' which is de facto uni-versal (that through which all ontic and ontological forms must 'pass'), but properly only in-the-last-instance (it reserves the relative autonomy of these secondary forms of causality). Such is the real—and not 'rational'—core of the dialectic, whether materialist or not. Althusser's 'error,' for example, is to have sought in Marx the rational, thus philosophical and idealist, core of the Hegelian dialectic, whereas, as with all philosophers, it is necessary to initially identify the real symptomatic core. Materialism, like finalism, technologism, and formalism, is expulsed from and by the DLI understood in its universal identity.

If the DLI is an original causality, without regional (naturalist or social) or fundamental and metaphysical model, then this contradicts materialism, even if the latter is a sort of immediate symptom of the immanent real, including neo-Platonism where causality has unilateral but restrained forms. In other words, its elucidation requires a minimum of 'speculation' on the general conditions of its internal possibility. Marx ascribes to the idea of a causality of the infra- on the superstructure without really elucidating it as the original imbrication ('cloning') of immanence and transcendence, as causality of the real on the ideal or the mixture of the ideal and effectivity. More radically still, the materialist context forces him to interpret this causality in an ontic-primary way, whereas, if it must render knowledge possible as identically theoretical and philosophical, it must be the causality of any grasping (having an 'intellective' rather than material-regional causality) or that which makes of the immanent real an experience of quasi-knowledge or, better still, of phenomenality.

If Marx has acquired a concept that begins to be viable concerning the immanence of the real, he stills proceeds in a metaphysical way, thus through a philosophical decision rather than an axiomatic act of 'primary ultimation.' Certain interpreters, like Henry, have developed this aspect of immanence but by forgetting the 'critical and revolutionary' aspect that conveys the DLI. Others, like Althusser, on the contrary have developed the aspect of transcendence, politics, and contradiction, but by completely forgetting the radical conditions of the DLI through idealism. As we said, *from this relative perspective* non-Marxism can seem like the exact identity of these two extreme interpreters, but an identity situated outside their interpretations. Non-Marxism is the determination-in-the-last-instance of these restrained and partial interpretations.

Thus the crucial problem of materialism is that it cannot theorize itself and needs an external theory of philosophical origin or an idealist complement under the form of a materialist position, for example the distinction of the category of materialism from that of the real—of matter—which must solve it. The DLI, which would have had to suffer if it had been fully deployed in its identity, requires the complement of a theory (of the) dialectic. Hence there has been a philosophical type of division between the DLI that passes for a material causality of the object (which is sometimes physico-mechanical) and a dialectic of contradiction that overdetermines it so as to render it intelligible and philosophically acceptable. Yet the DLI should not simply be the object of a theory but also its subject and its cause (we shall argue under a non-Hegelian form), the same type of causality of identity (of science and philosophy), an identity which is creative of knowledge, consequently without this identity (of-the-last-instance) having anything Hegelian about it. The problem is resolved when the DLI stops being thought in exteriority, according to the model of socio-economic causality, and when the infrastructure stops being posited as a matter or when it is understood as radical immanence, i.e. as One and vision-in-One. Because then without being itself a knowledge or a cognition (the real is foreclosed to this idealism), it is a given-without-givenness which is sufficient to itself, a real experience that is foreclosed to knowledge but capable of determining it outside of any materialist relation or any other relation whatsoever. The real is so heterogeneous to thought that it is capable of determining it as well as making it a cause through immanence (this will be the 'cloning' of the practical subject through the infrastructure on the basis of the material of the superstructure).

The 'real' solution to this problem of the DLI as object and cause of its own theory must avoid Hegelian idealism even more than materialism does. Neither cause in exteriority nor dialectical identity of contraries, the real is cause through immanence and determines the knowledge of its own syntax, of its causality, through a process that we shall call 'cloning.' In other words, the object X to be known must be, *on the one hand*, tested as radically immanent (i.e. seen-in-One, object of the vision-in-One) so as to be able to itself determine this form, and, *on the other hand*, it must be its own knowledge. This determination is a cloning through itself, but as One or immanent, of its knowledge. The material of the latter is furthermore given initially in its symptomatic form by philosophical and transcendent knowledge, through which it is given 'empirically' under philosophico-capitalistic conditions, a form which precisely must be determined-in-the-last-instance by itself. This is what needs to be explained more precisely.

There is the object X to be known. If it is affected by immanence or the DLI, i.e. seen-in-One, then it can clone itself on the basis of the material that its transcendence is. X is X-in-One, in the immanent mode of the One, and this now can be said transcendentally of X insofar as it is not immanent or is given the transcendence of the 'object' to be known. Thus in general, the DLI fully deployed is the causality that universally renders possible that which the object X itself determines, but *in-the-last-instance*, its own 'real' knowledge, i.e. the identity of the theoretical and the philosophical. X (or better still, for example, the concept of the DLI itself) is not known in exteriority, in an idealist way, but through itself, without this identity of the real and knowledge taking on the dialectical form (real = rational, etc.) since it takes on the form of DLI. There is no transcendent subject; knowledge is the subject, its 'own' subject if you will, as well as its object, but in the proximal 'last instance' of the real. It is as if the DLI required that matter (that of 'materialism') itself be known, capable of its own theory without passing through dialectical identity or some other philosophical apparatus that is destined to assure the reversibility of the object known and the knowledge of the object. Since it obviously cannot satisfy this self-knowledge, save by having recourse to an idealist and metaphysical complement which is called 'materialism' as position and system of categories, it must be admitted that it is not matter that can explain or render universal the identity of the DLI, i.e. the full usage of this concept, and that there is a *definite* contradiction between the DLI and materialism, above all dialectical materialism. When it is understood in its universal identity and when it is substituted for the dialectic everywhere and deprives it of every object, the DLI can be equivalent both to whichever object X—since it has the philosophical form of the world—and to itself. Its bearing is identically ontic and theoretical, for it is univocal for every object. When the DLI is the cause or immanent object of its own theory, we shall say that this theory *is* the *force (of) thought*, the theory of the force (of) thought being the same as the latter in-the-last-instance. It is as though 'labor power' were finally capable of its own 'proletarian' theory, without Hegelian idealism, or became the restrained model of the universal instance of the force (of) thought.

The object to be known, while remaining the known object, must therefore be capable of determining its knowledge. So as to avoid the idealism of the dialectic under its Hegelian form, it thus suffices that this object X be capable of radical immanence and not of the transcendence of matter—which is only possible if the DLI is the causality of the real base as radical immanence. This is to simultaneously respect the post-critical urgency of a knowledge of the object through the object itself along with the relative autonomy of the latter in relation to this knowledge. Knowledge is heterogeneous to the known object, but it is the latter which determines the former in-the-last-instance. The object X is identically—without being philosophically divided—cause of-the-last-instance of its knowledge and known object. Materialism simulates this property of the object on the 'base' of the vision-in-One. Basically the DLI and its identity have been divided into a material cause and a materialist or philosophical theory of this causality. *The identity of the DLI signifies that it is capable of its own knowledge without philosophical operation. The old problem of the possibility of knowledge is resolved not by the appeal to a transcendental subject or a ground but by the being-foreclosed of the real to knowledge, of every object to its knowledge, a being-foreclosed which does not render knowledge possible but determines it.*

Mechanism of the DLI: Cloning of the Superstructure

There is an unspecified given object X to be thought according to the DLI: what does this mean? The DLI is only understood on the basis of certain distinctions that are not regional and fundamental but equivalent with the real One.

1. The DLI must be posited on the terrain of the radical One, rather than that of Being and the existent, or even of the One-which-is. *Radical immanence can affect every X and constitute it on a 'real base,' but it is what subtends the DLI; it is not this X.* Any division between regional realities cannot explain it, and so it is unnecessary to fall back on such distinctions (for example, matter/ideology, whether or not this is redoubled as the distinction between the ideality of matter and the materiality of ideology). The One does not have such a content; it is thus universal or univocal and does more than 'surpass' whichever particular philosophical mechanism. The infrastructure is only determining in-the-last-instance if it has the uni-versality of immanence rather than that of fundamental and regional generality. But on this basis of the One-real, any material taken from the world or from universal capital can also be determining in-the-last-instance (from its knowledge), if axioms are added that specify this uni-versality of the real. If it does not have the properties of radical immanence, if it does not receive them, or if instead they are not 'given,' a regional object of the world or the world itself—in general both simul-

taneously—cannot ensure a DLI or act in this way on themselves so as to produce their own 'scientific' knowledge. Non-Marxism no longer supports an ontologico-transcendental and ontico-regional thematic, for example epistemo-logic. The epistemo-logical mixture, if it wishes to be able to determine its 'own' identically philosophical and theoretical knowledge in-the-last-instance, must change its status and pass through the radical immanence of the infrastructure.

It thus cannot be a question of taking X alone, since it is given in the context of its extraction, or with its native status and the pretentions that accompany it. In fact, X is necessarily presented in the capital-world, and if philosophy is the law of the world, then it is presented as philosophically posited or as explicitly philosophizable de facto. But the 'ontological' status of this givenness, whatever its particular philosophical treatment may be (empirical, idealist, phenomenological, etc.), prohibits it from fulfilling the DLI or satisfying it. It is necessary that X itself be given via the mode of the given-without-givenness or radical immanence so as to fulfill the conditions of the DLI: that it be reducible to a mode of the real, that it be seen-in-One or 'affected' by the vision-in-One. Marxist materialism is content with a half-solution and only posits the infrastructure—when it even wants to broach this problem—as immanence, as manufacturer or cause of immanence for its knowledge, via the mode that tolerates matter. The DLI is such that it has no meaning in the world and for matter appropriated via the world's mode of givenness.

2. Due to the universality of the DLI which we require, namely its univocality for every object taken from capital and having the uni(-)versal world-form or capital-form, X not only receives the status of infrastructure but also completely preserves that of superstructure. An unspecified regional and transcendent distinction, like that between productive forces

and relations of production or ideology, no longer has relevance at this level of univocality and will only regain it later as the object of specific axioms added to that of the DLI—Marxism thus being nothing but a model for non-Marxism. In this sense, the superstructure also must participate in this immanence, but properly this will only happen 'in-the-last-instance.' That means that X must *always also* be considered in its (relative) autonomy or in the transcendence with which it is given via the world, i.e. universal capitalism; but this transcendence (no longer ideological or restrained, but explicitly and thematically capitalistic) is now in turn affected by a different mode, a transcendental mode, by the immanence of the real which is now *said of it*. This is cloning.

3. Thus X's mode of givenness is considered in two ways: as given-without-givenness or radically immanent, a status that nullifies the reality of its transcendence and the consistency of its specific content; and as completely given-through-givenness via the mode of capitalistic transcendence and its (relative) autonomy. Nevertheless, X's two modes of givenness ground only one of them, without, however, their being synthesized. (Because the real immanence of X seen-in-One is not divided by capitalistic transcendence as it would be under a philosophical identity.) But everything remains as is or inalienable despite this capitalistic transcendence. Real immanence is said of this transcendence and afterwards receives another usage, which is transcendental and no longer simply real. Real immanence does not absorb or annihilate capitalistic transcendence; it is not *opposed* to it, but is capable of 'receiving' and determining it as *relative autonomy*. This immanence is so radical—and not 'absolute'—that it does not philosophically or phenomenologically reduce the transcendence of the world, for it neither denies nor limits it, but, on the contrary, gives it—certainly via its own mode: as the

being-given-without-givenness of transcendence itself which, while remaining 'absolute' or auto-positional in its order, acquires a relative autonomy in relation to the real. The concept of the 'relative autonomy' of the superstructure belongs to the 'logic' of the DLI and supposes real immanence, but is not deduced from the spontaneous transcendence of the world as given-through-givenness.

On the basis or ground of this 'reduction' of X, of this given-through-givenness which is itself given in turn without-givenness, radical immanence is equivalent to or for this transcendence *in its content or its own consistency of transcendence.* Therefore, because 'there is' an infrastructure, there is a superstructure that 'falls' under its efficacy. Why? Even reduced in its absolute pretention, X is not nullified, and furthermore it is no longer given only in an empirical and absolute way but lays claim to its autonomy henceforth 'in the interior' of its radical being-given and can do nothing but postulate a transcendent One that ensures its consistency as X or its relative autonomy, which in this way does not contradict its radical being-given. It is necessary not to forget that, due to its formalized generality, it is not only an ontico-ontological content but a way of being-given (without-givenness), and that real immanence participates in this transcendence of the world, but in the 'sterilized' or de-absolutized content of the latter. In a certain way this seems to limit the effect of immanence, but it no more limits it than the latter negatively affects transcendence. On the other hand, the real, being said also of this transcendence of X as irreducible and *added* core, has already fulfilled the role of a transcendental function (in relation to this transcendence) according to its essence of real. This is the operation that is called *cloning*: not of transcendence by immanence, but of the relative autonomy of the former by the latter beginning from the material that this transcendence is. This is necessary to the concept and to the possibility of a DLI. This is no longer a dialectical causality, even if there is a specific causality of X in relation to its own immanence (which obviously is not at its own origin but is that of the vision-in-One). This causality is possible because X-according-to-the-real or the 'base' now has the same immanent mode of being-given as X-according-to-the-world, due to the extent of the latter's transcendence. It has not lost its transcendence in general by losing the spontaneous sufficiency of the 'superstructure' or the world, but this is because it forms a specific content of the latter that exerts a causality which is merely 'occasional.'

4. *The specific ontic content of X is spontaneously confused with a transcendence, thus with another transcendence doubled from that of the world which would be reduced.* More accurately, the immanent real 'separates' X *and its transcendence* from each other by unilateralizing them. It is not necessary to separate X—under the pretext of immanence—into its mode of being-given and its specific content, risking a new philosophical reduction of a separation between the ideal and the ontico-empirical real. The vision-in-One does not reduce the transcendence of X in this sense of reduction but simply unilateralizes it in an immanent way. On the one hand, X is now given via the mode of being-given-without-givenness, foreclosed to itself as transcendent and not simply as sufficient. *Foreclosed* however does not indicate a new operation of transcendence taking X for an object. This being-foreclosed is precisely immanent or obtained by radical immanence alone. In other words, the transcendence-world (of X) is unilateralized or ineffective on X in its radical mode of being-given. On the other hand, the transcendence of X is not nullified or overcome in its consistency, but it is inefficacious on the 'immanent' X—this is a completely 'real reduction.' Rendered inefficacious yet subsisting with X, with the content with which it forms an in-

divisible mixture, this transcendence does not deny the real immanence of the infrastructure, does not limit it by dividing it, but is satisfied with still being offered to it (to what has already given it) in its neutrality. What is offered is not the content (of) X separated from its transcendence, but instead the content of transcendence itself, sterilized yet given as an 'object' that calls for a transcendental function of the real or provokes its cloning. This is not the only content (of) X that would be 'saved' from real immanence, initially because everything is given by the vision-in-One; and also because the transcendence of X is not destroyed as such but sterilized as is. If the real separates something in X (which must be considered as real in order to assume a DLI), this separation is a being-separated rather than a division, a being-foreclosed of X in relation to its native or extracted transcendence, its sufficiency. Consequently, this transcendence does not combine with the immanence of X, neither limits nor contradicts it, but can without contradiction solicit it or squeeze a transcendental function from it, or be the material for the operation of cloning that realizes it. This is why the *real* One can assume a transcendental function alongside X; not alongside its spontaneous worldly transcendence (absolute or sufficient) which is nullified, but alongside its sterilized or reduced content. There is thus no contradiction in the fact that the real as immanence assumes a transcendental function determined by X's content of transcendence.

The uni-versality of the DLI and the real contains an element of indifference, but not a formalism. Because they are precisely indifferent to the mixture of form and matter, they are not determinable like formalism is. Rigorously, it would be a question of an axiomatic-transcendental formalization. This indifference is their being-foreclosed to the world but is not properly speaking a formalism, even if they are uni-versally equal for every object-in-the-world. It is so little a formalism that this 'diagram' of non-Marxism is rather like a schema specifiable by the capital-world and supposing the support of new axioms. The act of non-Marxism is initially the being-given of the uni(-)versality of capitalism and its theory rather than the attempt to acquire them step-by-step through the complexification of axioms.

Identically Scientific and Philosophical Theory of the DLI

After the preceding explanations, the DLI is deduced from the radical immanence of the real alone, from the uni-versal concept of infrastructure (insofar as it is thus equivalent to the superstructure and the latter is taken into account), never from the ontic models of science or the ontological models of philosophy. The scientific and the philosophical, that which the DLI is capable of producing in their identity of-the-last-instance, are neither on the side of the One alone, being deduced as such solely from it, nor on the side of the world alone and its epistemo-logical auto-knowledge. There is no longer the scientific-of-the-last-instance on the side of science (*'la' science*) separated alone, nor the philosophical-of-the-last-instance, with which the former is radically identical, on the side of philosophy (*'la' philosophie*) separated alone. The DLI makes it possible to bypass these antinomies which are simply philosophical divisions. There is the vision-in-One and what it receives or rather 'gives' via its mode, the epistemo-logical mixture of philosophy and science in their indissoluble combinations.

If we wish to formalize it, the epistemo-logical mixture is presented as the other of X (X being the mixed or philosophical form; the other being science as other of philosophy but always included in the mixture and giving it its scope of epistemo-logical difference). In the DLI's operation, this given mixture is not presented by the real itself, which lacks the means to do so. However, the vision-in-One completely presents it as One or identity and then fulfills a transcendental role alongside its content of the other of X. The One does not produce of itself the scientific other, which is a mixture. It does not clone the scientific and the philosophical separately as if it isolated them within their mixture, which it divided. It needs to (receive-) give the other of X, the groundless block of the epistemo-logos, which is not the scientific and the philosophical pure and separated, but the concrete in which they alone have existence. We will avoid making the structure of the DLI fall back on the duality of science and philosophy, which is itself nothing but a contingent material, saying for example that the vision-in-One gives the in-itself or the real immanence of X while ensuring its heterogeneity, which is thus a scientific type of relation to X; and that the transcendental cloning of X is a relation of the philosophical type of the real to X. No doubt, we would then have a relation to X that would have no resemblance to X and would thus be a relation of theoretical knowledge in general, a relation that is not an image of X. But in fact, science and philosophy are initially given in-mixture, and the real can only clone the latter. Since it is not the One that constitutes it, these disciplines or these two forms of knowledge cannot be effectively deduced from it or presupposed as already existing in the real. The epistemo-logical mixture is the only material for cloning, and the clone is always clone (of) a mixture, not an abstract and separated term. For this reason, the clone is the identity of a double or a mixture and here an identity of-the-last-instance of the scientific and the philosophical. Because it is not specifically scientific or philosophical and because it is foreclosed to all knowledge, the vision-in-One can only clone their identity on the basis of the material of the mixture that the capital-world provides for it.

The DLI is thus neither the dialectic nor the synthesis of science and philosophy supposedly separated in external and contingent relations. The real determines the philosophical and the scientific in-the-last-instance as the 'same' identity of-the-last-instance, inalienable and indeterminable by philosophy and science such as they exist in the transcendence of the capital-world. In other words, it does not acquire a scientific universal and a philosophical universal separately, but in their identity (of) mixture (rather than mixed identity). It is not possible to combine them a posteriori after their works and their life in the world. That they are universals in non-Marxism does not mean that, on the contrary, they are pure and separated. There is a universal matrix of the scientific (and) the philosophical such that they are non-separated. The DLI does not divide contraries or dialectically unite them, but unites them without-unity or unites them through-identity. This is what we call their *unified theory*, here namely of theory and (philosophical) pragmatics. Their unitary theory in and through the capital-world supposes a double intervention by one of the parts of philosophy. When the DLI or the real replaces philosophical synthesis, science and philosophy then play 'a fair game,' which is only possible in their identity of-the-last-instance and not in their juxtaposition. This equality, this suspension of philosophical synthesis, is never their separation from one another. In the identity (of the) mixture, science is liberated by itself, it escapes from the tutelage of philosophy, which does not signify that it is 'finally' separated from the latter.

The complete understanding of this mechanism supposes that the epistemo-logical mixture of science and philosophy is provided or 'decided' by the capital-world, which, having become a real base, being immanent in-One, determines its own identically theoretical (and) philosophical knowledge in-the-last-instance, a knowledge (of) self of the epistemo-logos in the proximal last instance of the real. X is not an unspecified existent, but concretely the capital-world form that contains a program for the knowledge and usage of the existent. It is thus universal capitalism that, seen-in-One or in-infrastructure (the equivalent of its historical-materialist interpretation, the possibility of its immanent radical being), must assume the function of real immanent base determining its knowledge or its theory in-the-last-instance (under the form, we shall say, of the force (of) thought or of the Stranger, a more radical, more universal concept of the proletariat). Because of its status as independent base of its material, of science as well as philosophy, it determines an intrinsic identity of the latter without domination. There is no longer a reversal of philosophical primacy by science. Science and philosophy can only be equal in-the-last-instance and insofar as the real is foreclosed to the one and the other. The real is not their *commonality*, by analogy or ontological univocity, but their identity of-the-last-instance. It is non-philosophy and non-science, but the knowledge to which it gives rise or determines is the non-philosophy-of-science in the sense that the philosophy-of-science, the epistemo-logos, has lost its synthetic capacity. Science can be liberated from philosophical authority, but not from philosophy, since it is related to the latter under the non-philosophical condition of the givenness of the real.

The DLI is not only one of the essential objects of non-Marxist 'theory' but also the causality of the real, not on this theory, but on the epistemo-logical mixture; it causes the constitution of this theory beginning from this mixture. Non-Marxist theory is no longer suspended by a particular philosophy; it no longer considers the DLI in exteriority but complies with the latter as with the causality that produces or determines it, and it is even its exercise.

Thus deployed in its concept and usage, the DLI, or at least the identity of the DLI and the dialectic, seems like the materialist dialectic's real core. Marxism remains divided in the dyad of historical materialism (–> DLI) and dialectical materialism (–> philosophy), interpreted in a premature manner, as we have seen, as that of science and philosophy. Rather than complexifying it through the effects of theoretical interventions, which only multiply divisions, it is necessary to deprive Marxism not only of 'expressive totality' (Althusser), which is responsible for ensuring the mediation of Marxism and the real, the concrete grasp of the former on the latter; it must be deprived also of the useless postulate of philosophy as unifying synthesis which is supposedly constitutive.

Chapter 9

What Can Non-Philosophy Do?

Translated by Ray Brassier

I. The Infinite End of Philosophy

Our contemporary situation is, as ever, complex. It harbors numerous contrasts. But one of its most telling characteristics is that of a bustling philosophical activity that masks a fundamental indifference to philosophy. Were we to set aside those distortions that are a function of historical perspective, we would see that this situation is perfectly normal, but a superficial awareness or consciousness of this phenomenon is particularly acute at the present time. Is this indicative of a lack of interest? A lack of purpose? Indifference? Unlike their predecessors, who were directly preoccupied with philosophy itself, modern philosophers have tended to be more preoccupied with their relation to philosophy as it is mediated across historical distance. We no longer practice philosophy naïvely and spontaneously from within itself, as though it were a second nature or a habitat. Kant shattered this spontaneity and bequeathed to us a new problem: that of the *use* of philosophy. What are we to do with metaphysics from now on? It is as though we have been burdened with a suffocating legacy—we

This essay first appeared in English translation in *Angelaki: Journal of the Theoretical Humanities* 8.2 (2003), 169-189.

have inherited scraps that we do not know what to do with. Are we supposed to reprocess or even recycle these scraps of thought? Is it a question of the ecology of thought—a thought that no longer knows how to dispose of its products? There is something of this in our legacy and in our overburdened memory. But why does modern man formulate the problem of his legacy by wondering how to manage something that sometimes appears as a shortage and at other times as a surplus? Perhaps it is necessary to reformulate the problem of our relation to the tradition and begin by putting the latter to one side. Is it then a question of the 'end of philosophy'?

But is the expression 'end of philosophy,' or 'end of metaphysics,' not part of this same cumbersome legacy? Let us use the expression 'without-philosophy' instead, but only on condition that we ascribe the lack or absence of philosophy to man now understood as 'man-in-person,' and that we re-examine these problems from this new angle. To understand this change in problematic, we have to go back to the origins of the law of philosophy.

'End of philosophy' is a philosophical expression not only by virtue of its formulation but also through its meaning and as a matter of principle. It expresses philosophy in its ultimate possibility—winding around itself, gathering itself and withdrawing from thought. Philosophy encloses itself, consummates itself as a form of technique, leaving behind an empty space for a new experience of thought. Heidegger and Derrida have added certain important nuances to this schema. But it still has to be understood as expressing the essence of philosophy: an auto-positional essence indefinitely closing on itself, while missing or exceeding itself by a difference intrinsic to that identity, so that it never fully achieves either a perfect closure or a perfect opening. This is not to say that auto-positioning or auto-beginning always fails, or fails as a matter of principle. It fails only to the same degree that it succeeds because this structure—specular in nature—is divided by a difference or alterity that remains subordinated to its identity, the whole forming a dyadic/triadic structure that is equally and simultaneously open and closed.

It may be that this structure is never manifested in a pure state within the history of philosophy, that it is always somewhat unbalanced depending on whether the emphasis is on identity or alterity. Nevertheless, it forms the principal core, the minimal invariant that must be presupposed as operative in any doctrine of a philosophical or systematic type. This core defines philosophy as a 'theoreticist idealism' or 'idealist theoreticism.' This is not the name of a particular doctrine but another name for the essence of philosophy as such. In other words, every philosophy, however it comes to be realized, is bound to a specularity that it mistakes for the real, bound to a primacy and priority of theory as reflection of that real—the two together constituting 'speculation.' Different doctrines may vary this structure but they 'economize' philosophy's presence and absence in such a way that its absence remains intrinsic to its continuous presence. It is always philosophical mastery that decides—without deciding—about philosophy's end: for example (since we are talking about speculation) about its overcoming or internalizing *Aufhebung*.

The unitary and sufficient presupposition which is intrinsic to philosophy's self-relation (and which fuelled theoreticist idealism from the Greeks to Hegel) was merely somewhat weakened by the various kinds of deconstruction when they began to acknowledge that philosophy's auto-closure was simultaneously enabled and hindered by an alterity—but an alterity that they in turn continued to presuppose as sufficient or absolute, rather than as a radical alterity or alterity in-person.

This amounted to yet another division (albeit one that was now uneven) between philosophy and an alterity that is partially extra-philosophical yet that continues to ratify philosophy's basic sufficiency. The latter is precisely what an anonymous alterity of this kind is incapable of revoking.

II. The Real or Identity-in-Person

Non-philosophy is not a return to identity or to its primacy in the wake of twentieth-century philosophy's orgy of alterity and difference. It is not some sort of reaction. Perhaps it is another identity altogether that is at issue here. Identity-in-person has never yet been attained. Identity has only ever been aimed at as though it were homologous with an object, one that might be used for various ends. Philosophical thought is directed toward identity intentionally, via transcendence as *epekeina* rather than as *meta*. Thus, it is obliged to make certain corrective adjustments in that practice of objectivation. Identity becomes the object of desire rather than of knowledge; it conditions the latter without falling under it, etc. *Nevertheless, it remains inseparable from transcendence as deployed through the* meta, *from eidetic being—as though it constituted an uneven half tacked on to this transcendence.* Whence the fact that the *epekeina*, which is absolute transcendence, remains relatively dependent upon the *meta*, which is relative transcendence. Like desire, philosophy is ambitious, it is the enjoyment of the absolutely other; but the weakness of the absolute resides in its point of departure and in its process, which consists in an absolutization of experience.

Non-philosophy is founded in another experience of identity. It conceives of identity precisely as that to which it is impossible to direct thought towards intentionally—whether as object or horizon. It conceives of identity as something that cannot be attained via transcendence. This is identity-in-person, the One in flesh and blood, which does not tolerate either internal transcendence or external, operational transcendence. It is not the object of a construction or of a philosophical desire deployed within the realm of what is operationally intuitable. It is the philosopher, not just philosophy, who is from the outset (albeit not definitively) put out of play as a *deus ex machina*. This is why non-philosophy simulates philosophy in its beginning, but does so through a different gesture. Philosophy begins and remains within itself, within its own immanence, by presupposing itself—but in such a way as to be capable of minimizing and re-integrating its own presuppositions, which are gathered up in transcendence. The immanence of philosophy is complex, split into two: it is at once thematic and functional, requiring various gestures of transcendence or presupposition, but ones that can ultimately be minimized and re-integrated, or that are already directly amenable to integration (Hegel). This is characteristic of the auto-encompassing style of philosophy.

By way of contrast, although non-philosophy also begins in immanence and remains within it, it does not take the form of a self-encompassing movement in which identity merely functions to close or seal the circle. In non-philosophy, identity as such is no longer a function of anything else. No matter how much a functional identity simulates the real, or engenders real effects, it invariably dissolves in the only available reality: the reality of the system as the meta-stable, self-encompassing reality of philosophical desire. The question then is whether it is enough to restrict oneself to the construction—and thereby to the deconstruction—of a system of philosophical desire; or whether—in complete contrast—we should try to elaborate a theory of it instead. Let us continue our analysis.

III. The Transcendental or the Separated Middle: A Theory of Alterity

Identity-in-person is a primary name. There are others, such as man-in-person. Once it has been rigorously defined, rather than given over to the realm of unitary, metaphysical or anthropological generality; once it has been axiomatically determined rather than presupposed through vague theses or statements; what we are calling 'man' as identity is so in-consistent, so devoid of essence, as to constitute *a hole in nothingness itself, not just in being*. It is a blind-spot for philosophical auto-reflection, which now assumes the mantle of nothingness, now being, or shifts from one to the other. The concept of auto-reflection applies equally to the most ancient philosophies and to modern ones. It is indicative of theoreticist idealism and speculation as the essence of philosophical systems. Yet not only is the One-in-One foreign to all ontological or linguistic consistency, it is also foreign to all inconsistency. It is the without-consistency. Man-in-person or identity can be defined, in terms that are homologous with the simultaneously excluded and included middle that systematically opens and closes philosophy, as the *identity-without-middle* or better still as *the separated middle*, which is neither included nor excluded, neither consistent nor inconsistent, etc. It is neither of these two predicates as opposed to one another or as synthesized into a third term. In other words, no set of dyadic philosophical predicates is appropriate to 'man-in-person'—which is not to say the latter is 'ineffable,' as is objected by philosophers who assume that to state something about X or Y is to attribute a predicate to a subject and thereby to affect the real through language. The separated middle is neither included nor excluded...but not because it is both at once, in the manner of a philosophical synthesis. It is *separated*...from inclusion and exclusion as such, separated from the kind of relation involved in those dualities with which thought traditionally operates. It is a rule of philosophy that the 'neither…nor…,' which appears to exclude predicates from the real, actually reintroduces them into it by assuring us that it is 'at once' one and the other, with the obvious proviso that this double negation be included within the final result. In non-philosophy, however, the 'neither…nor…' is definitive from the outset because it expresses the being-separated proper to identity, or to the separated-in-person.

In other words, this being-separated, which we will later refer to as the *other than*…, is not an attribute of identity, analytically or synthetically contained within the latter. Rather, it is its transcendental aspect, which as real is invisible. This transcendental aspect is not a *property* of identity but is instead the very same thing as identity, or the function of *relation to*… which identity is always able to assume. Nevertheless, it is only insofar as it is real or immanent that identity can constitute a transcendental alterity, rather than the other way round. It may seem strange to think identity as the middle, but this is an example of a philosophical necessity—in this instance, the way in which identity regularly functions as the third fundamental term in philosophy—being reconfigured non-philosophically.

How are we to conceive of this transcendental alterity that is proper to the real as identity-in-person? Let us consider for a moment dialectical identity as that which differentiates itself from itself, becomes other than itself, etc. Alterity affects it or belongs to its complex essence even if it is surmounted or overcome by identity. Identity is at once a 'subordinate part' and the whole, while alterity is a subordinate part of the whole, the two together forming a continuous plane, or something susceptible to further dialecticization. Let us suppose now that instead of finding alterity at the heart of identity, one encountered there only identity itself—identity as the flesh of the One itself rather than as the remainder of a gesture of abstraction. Such abstraction would reduce identity to something still less than an envelope, something that is not even a topological plane or pure surface but more like a logically formalized term or symbol. Yet identity-in-person is not a symbol but an identity whose own identity constitutes its phenomenon, its 'flesh.' Real identity is impoverished, impoverished to an extent that is unimaginable for philosophy, but it is not impoverished because all alterity has been abstracted from it or because it has been stripped bare through a process of alienation. It is indeed articulated through a symbol, and its effects are in turn articulated through a play of symbols, but to confuse the real with its symbol is precisely the mistake of theoreticist idealism and the root of all philosophical illusion.

This confusion begins when, without one's noticing it, identity-in-person is spontaneously imagined to be a bare term, a pure signifier devoid of signification. In fact, identity-in-person has no need of signification and is not of the order of the signifier. The real is not just what is impossible for the symbol; it is of an entirely other order and capable of determining a sign as symbol. This is enough to distinguish non-philosophy from psychoanalysis. Identity did not undergo the 'linguistic turn,' and neither does the symbol when it is determined by identity. There is a sense in which identity-in-person is the real-transcendental cause—rather than the condition of possibility—of symbolization in a way that precludes the assumption that symbols are given ready-made, or provided via a symbolizing givenness. In other words, any philosophical coupling of terms directed at the One, or even at being, may be used to name real identity, provided those terms undergo a symbolic abstraction (but one that bears only on the symbol and not also on the real). As for the real itself, it is already abstract without there having been an operation of abstraction.

Having nothing but its own being-manifest—which is not even an essence—as content, identity cannot strictly speaking act or exert a direct positive causality. Since it is without essence, it can be neither active nor passive—no more so than it can be both at once, as though to compensate for this supposed deficiency. It is incapable of functioning as motor for a dialectic. It is 'negative' rather than negational; a non-sufficient cause, rather than one that is sufficient and essential. Yet this quasi-sterility, this neutrality without return or compensation, in no way prevents it from taking into account or 'cloning' philosophy as a reduced datum or material. This taking into account does not cause it to exit from itself; it does not constrain it to act. It is separated without that separation eating into it or affecting its essence. At the same time, since this being-separated directly expresses identity or radical immanence, it is brought forth, so to speak, by the vision-in-One as the latter takes into account what is offered by philosophy. Immanent knowledge is *other than*...philosophical. We must replace Levinas' *otherwise than*, which is still anonymous and pertains to absolute transcendence, with *other than*...: an adjective rather than a noun, but one that has been raised to the status of a primary name for the real or man-in-person.

Of course, philosophy also invokes a One-Other as the object that provides the supreme instance of absolute transcendence or *epekeina*. But there the situation is complicated by the fact that the nature of this object is still that of the philosophical combination in its topological form as infinite, self-enclosed Mœbius strip. The radical One, by way of contrast, is initially in-One without the Other belonging to it. Consequently, it is Other only to the extent to which it is Other-in-Other or Other than...In philosophy, the combinatory structure or system continues to predominate so that philosophy can only posit the One-Other as a term in the guise of something that remains an 'ideological' artifact: an effect or result that has been abstracted from the process through which it was produced. In non-philosophy, on the contrary, the One as such is not subordinated to any thing or structure because it is genuinely independent and has no need of such support. But at the same time the One is the Other-in-Other, which by virtue of this fact also acquires a radical autonomy. We could say that, as in philosophy, the Other is still first, but that it no longer has any primacy. Alternatively, and more precisely, we could say that primacy and priority always go hand in hand, but that in philosophy they are actually subordinated to a combinatory structure which is the true locus of power and independence; one that secretly enjoys a kind of hyper-primacy and is deployed in the realm of operational transcendence. In non-philosophy, however, the One-Other subsists without being subordinated in an idealist fashion to the syntax of this operational transcendence and its combinatory-izing economy. Both primacy and priority are shorn of the equivocal, self-doubling nature which is characteristic of speculative identity. Primacy and priority go together but as the real that is also capable of assuming the function of transcendental or other than…for philosophy. They go together as the real that is independent but that is also primary.

Rather than dividing and doubling the One-Other by itself, or infinitely multiplying it, non-philosophy simplifies it. In philosophy, the One is never purely and simply 'One,' unless it is a mere symbol, as it is in the principle of identity, in which it is already doubled by itself. Philosophy invariably doubles and multiplies it, as in the neo-Platonists' hierarchy of Ones, or the more or less mediated identity of (difference and) identity. It is imperative not to confuse the One of philosophy, which is the *One (of the) One*, with the One of non-philosophy, which is the One-in-One or the One-in-person, the One in flesh and blood. Is the latter also multiplied, either by itself or by being divided? Or does it amount to an impoverishment, an abstraction-subtraction, a One–1? The expression 'One-in-One' or 'vision-in-One' indicates the absence of any operation that would define the latter; the fact that it is not inscribed within an operational space or more powerful structure; its immanence *in* itself rather than *to* anything else; its naked simplicity as never either exceeding or lacking, because it is the only measure required, but one that is never a self-measurement, one that measures nothing as long as there is nothing to measure.

IV. Producing a Program of Existence

If there is a non-philosophical program, it consists in appropriating philosophy or the world (in a broadened sense of the term).

Why does non-philosophy invariably appear in the form of a program or a project, one that irritates people because it never seems to be realized? The answer is that, although it has nothing to do with a program in its essential or practical aspect, its inessential aspect (which is precisely the philosophical aspect non-philosophy assumes through its 'material') makes it appear as though it does. This programmatic appearance is unavoidable but it is no more than an appearance, in other words, something we will call a program-without-programming or at the very least a program for de-programming. What matters is knowing whether or not it will be possible to overcome this appearance and to acknowledge it as such. What follows explores part of this program, guided by the theme of non-philosophical practice and what it is capable of, with regard to philosophy but also in the eyes of philosophy.

Why a 'non-philosophy'? Philosophy is so varied, so fickle, that it has already criticized itself in an infinite variety of ways, already exhibited such a degree of metamorphic plasticity as to disqualify any attempt to reduce it to a single invariant of thought. Was there any point in trying to do so? The question "what *is* non-philosophy?" must be replaced by the question about what it can and cannot *do*. To ask what it can do is already to acknowledge that its capacities are not unlimited. This question is partly Spinozist: no one knows what a body can do. It is partly Kantian: circumscribe philosophy's illusory power, the power of reason or the faculties, and do not extend its sufficiency in the shape of another philosophy. It is also partly Marxist: how much of philosophy can be transformed through practice, how much of it can be withdrawn from its 'ideological' use? And finally, it is also partly Wittgensteinian: how can one limit philosophical language through its proper use?

But these apparent philosophical proximities and family resemblances are only valid up to a point. That point is called the real—determination-in-the-last-instance, the unilateral duality, etc.—which is to say, all of non-philosophy in-person. In other words, these kinds of comparisons are devoid of meaning, or at best profoundly misleading, because non-philosophy is 'performative' and exhausts itself as an immanent practice rather than as a program.

The answer to the question "what are we to do with philosophy?" must already have been given in the form of the question "what can non-philosophy do?" The latter provides a rigorous formulation of the former by delineating a space within which it can enjoy a certain pertinence without being allowed to get carried away with itself. It was Heidegger who unleashed the absurd delirium of 'total questioning.' But his work is seldom read right through to the end, to the point where the primacy of the question is overturned in favor of a primacy of the answer. We can radicalize him and affirm the primacy of the answer over questions, which we will characterize as merely 'primary' and as pertaining to the beginning but not to the real. Conversely, however, the answer cannot be primary in some dogmatic sense; it can only impose or determine a way of answering.

Non-philosophy is usually interrogated about its efficacy, about what it can achieve in terms of *effects*. "What are the politics of non-philosophy?" "What are its ethical consequences?" Without realizing it, such questions harbor a whole host of assumptions and prejudices, which is not to say that we have an excuse for ignoring them. But it is important that we not allow ourselves to be intimidated by these kinds of questions or objections. They are only valid for philosophy; they reiterate its bad habits in order to reassure it. This way of formulating questions imposes a double limitation. On the one hand, it assumes a linear and above all a unitary causality in terms of causes and effects that are ultimately reversible and 'Euclidean' (one cause, one effect). This is to assume a form of empiricism: causality is specified through the nature of its effects, a regional nature that is carved out from the world. What would a 'non-Euclidean' action be like? One that acted upon the world as such, rather than on part of it or on a sector of philosophy? This is a problem that involves a change in methods and objectives, a change in the nature of the object, rather than a mere change in scale or the choice of another region traced from an already-given section of the world. The entire theory of causality will have to be transformed in its meaning and bearing relative to philosophy. There may well be political as well as other kinds of effects of non-philosophy, but does this justify such a crude formulation of the question?

In this regard, it was Marxism that first cast suspicion on any attempt to provide a slightly more nuanced analysis of the political problem by encouraging the belief that such attempts secretly sought to obscure the class struggle. Yet it is not clear whether non-philosophy can be appraised in terms of a 'program,' or whether it consummates itself in something like a program. In this regard, on the contrary, the Marxist notion of class struggle paved the way for an acknowledgement of the fact that politics has a real content, albeit one which is not political according to superficial, factual criteria. Similarly, just as man does not produce his existence but his means of existence, *he does not produce his political existence or nature but his means of political existence.* If he can wage class struggle through politics, he can 'wage politics' through the class struggle. Which is why a slightly more rigorous (and probably already 'non-Marxist') understanding of Marx's formula requires us to effect a unilateral distinction between the political struggle and a struggle that is constitutive of its subjects, a struggle whose universality envelops a possible but non-necessary reference (unless it be the general necessity of referring to a material) to politics or any other worldly activity. This is the way in which subjects produce themselves as means (organons) of political existence.

Marx's formula is thus in need of urgent rectification, the better to maximize its novelty and scope: *man-in-person is given as the real presupposition on the basis of which subjects produce themselves as means of existence with the participation of their political existence in the world.* Consequently, we should distinguish between (1) man-in-person as the real presupposition whose nature has never been either political or anything else; (2) the political existence of subjects in the world; and finally, (3) the subject proper as 'means of existence'—a subject whose rigorous, quasi-mathematical formulation clearly marks it out as an organon constituted with the aid of that against which it struggles, i.e. existence. The aim of this 'dualysis' of Marx's formula is to lay low the theoreticist idealism of philosophy, which levels out in a unitary continuum man-in-person and his duality as subject, together with the existence in terms of which this structure is interpreted whenever the question of political action, or of other effects, is raised. Thus, we interpret 'class-struggle' as a struggle that is constitutive of subjects (but not of man-in-man), but in a way that reinserts it into the apparatus as an articulatory hinge, instead of placing it either at the center or the periphery. Of course, struggle constitutes the essence of subjects and finds support in the *existence of classes* but it cannot be reduced to the latter. It is as subjects that humans become indistinguishable from classes, but this is precisely so as to be better able to distinguish themselves from classes. Whence this corollary: humans do not produce their non-philosophical existence or essence, but only a program that functions as a means of their existence.

Non-philosophy needs to be resituated in the context of the struggle against philosophy—or at least against philosophy understood as theoreticist idealism, which transcends any particular philosophical position and prevents the elaboration of a unified theory of philosophy and (for example) politics. It should not be circumscribed from the outset within the narrow ambit of 'politics' [*la-politique*] in the restricted sense, which encourages all sorts of illusion. As we shall see, it is the transcendental yet practical dimension of non-philosophy that accounts for the erroneous or spontaneously philosophical character of the demand that it have political or other effects within the contemporary situation. For the real problem is not how to intervene in the world of philosophy, such as it supposedly subsists in-itself, or how to transform it from within. The problem is how to use philosophy so as to effect a real transformation of the subject in such a way as to allow it to break the spell of its bewitchment by the world and enable it to constitute itself through a certain struggle with the latter. The goal is not to effect a specular doubling or duplication of the world, thereby reinforcing its grip, but to elaborate a new order, that of the radical subjectivity of the Stranger as subject who is in-struggle by definition. Thus, what had been an aporia for philosophy, but also partially for Marxism—the possibility of man's alienation in the world (an alienation that is now merely partial and only involves the Stranger-subject, not man's essence-without-essence), along with the corresponding possibility of man's dis-alienation—is finally resolved here. The unilateral duality of man and the world-subject or Stranger-subject finally resolves this aporia.

V. Practice of Theory

The question now is whether practice can have any meaning other than as a purely theoretical practice. The economy of theory and practice harbors all sorts of traps for the unwary because it is intra-philosophical and follows the classic distinctions, distinctions that comprise both division *and* identity, and that give rise to self-encompassing indecisions and hesitations between theory and practice—exchanges and ambiguities, mutual trespasses and territorial disputes, oppositions and contradictions. This kind of distribution pertains not only to philosophy but also to experience, injecting it with its vicious circles and interminable debates. The solutions proposed by philosophy are well known, so we will not go over them here. They have been a staple of philosophy from Plato to Marx and beyond.

Non-philosophy introduces order into this combinatory confusion, but not in a philosophical manner. It does not oppose its own practice (which is theoretical) to philosophical theory, as though the former were at last the true transformative practice while the latter remained a merely contemplative theory. There is no question of reiterating the kind of intra-philosophical distinctions that Marxism popularized through the use of opposition and contradiction. Here once again the unilateral duality governs the relation to philosophy, and it does not reshuffle philosophical distinctions but instead 'simplifies' them by suspending a redundant postulate, a suspension that allows us to attain a radical universality. This is why we speak of practice being 'of' or 'in' theory: far from being opposed to it, practice is able to determine-in-the-last-instance the philosophical forms of theory and their combination with empirical practice. To determine-in-the-last-instance is to posit the real-transcendental identity of a subject who is structured like a *mixture* (rather than a combination) of the theoretical stance and the practical stance, but in such a way that neither stance trespasses upon the other's terrain. The unilateral duality is the practical essence that must be pitted against philosophy's theoreticist idealism. But it is certainly not opposed to theory, implying rather a simplifying concentrate of philosophical combinations. Where philosophy mixes theory and practice according to the invariant of combination, non-philosophy associates them without synthesis or analysis, without a mediating term. The transcendental identity or essence of the subject is not a mediating agency or third term countable within the same operational space as the duality of the combination. The subject's transcendental identity provides the reason why non-philosophy can be an identity *for*…philosophy, which is to say, its 'dualysis.' Although the subject is radically identical in its essence, it can only concretely effectuate identity with the aid of a variety of philosophical solutions that delineate the contours of the world, which the subject accompanies and which continuously fill out its non-saturated being.

Ultimately then, identity as cause of practice is commensurate with its non-consistency. Practice is the only stance that is heterogeneous to every other activity because it is univocal for all of them, give or take their determination-in-the-last-instance. But here it is practice in theory and relative to it, because theory is the only practice of first science, which is constituted by the stances of science and philosophy.

VI. Transforming the Site of Transformation

Non-philosophy transforms materials, but these materials are both taken from the world *and* possess the general form of the world. Yet the philosophical requirement of efficacy postulates a universal site for philosophy in the world. Here we encounter an initial assumption that expresses a unitary and levelling conception of action, which is supposed to affect only one region of experience and to exhaust itself in it. This quasi-universal empiricism of action and practice is philosophically self-evident: it seems obvious that all production consists in transforming a material while staying on the same level as it, remaining content with distending the general convertibility of the realms implicated in practice. Even when structured by Difference as such, rather than merely specific differences as in Marxism, practices are still not heterogeneous enough to exceed the world, to which they return once the latter has been given its widest possible definition, which is precisely in terms of Difference and its alterity.

By way of contrast, if practice is conceived in terms of unilateral duality, which is the syntax proper to the strict immanence of the real as other than…the world, then this non-representative causality of determination-in-the-last-instance presupposes a radical distinction between the order of reality and the order of syntax, so that neither one of these encompasses the other. Once it has been founded upon a non-agency or non-realm like the real, the conception of agencies, realms or orders eliminates every facile dialectic, no matter how deeply entrenched in representation. It institutes a transformation of the material as production of a new agency that cannot be ultimately reabsorbed into that material, an agency that does not consummate itself within the order of the world. The subject produced in this way is one that emerges beyond the world but who nevertheless continues to refer to the world as a form of necessary yet secondary and entirely occasional causality. Such is the transcendence specific to the subject insofar as it stands beyond all philosophical transcendence, not so much through an excess of hyperbolic transcendence as through an immanent grasp or cloning of the latter. Cloning is an operation of radical immanence insofar as it takes on a transcendental relation to a given datum that has the form of the world, transforming that datum into a material by virtue of the very fact that it is *other than*...it. Because the agency of the subject exists-(as a)-Stranger, the site of production remains distinct from the world, announcing itself (among other things) as the future-in-person, utopia-in-person, or the transcendental city of multitudes. Thus, practice first transforms the very site of the world's transformation and effects what we might legitimately call its 'radical' displacement.

If we want to formulate correctly the question of the effects of non-philosophy, we must have 'exited' from the world without first having had to enter into it in order to leave it. We have to think according to the real—which does not mean without the world—rather than according to the world. Non-philosophy is entirely oriented towards the future, and, more fundamentally, it is entirely oriented towards a utopia of the real. It is produced as the *identity* of transformation and chooses to abandon not the world as such but rather the site of the world. It is a new way of relating to things-according-to-the-world, one that no longer considers them in terms of the previous ways of relating to entities within the horizon of the world as something simply presupposed. If things are inseparable from the world, it is not on account of philosophical desire but because the world functions as their a priori mode of givenness, such that it is the site of their transformation that has to change.

As a result, there will be a change in the meaning and scope of alienation and appropriation. They no longer pertain to man in general in his anthropological essence but only to the subject conceived on the basis of man-in-person, who is neither alienable nor inalienable and too inconsistent to be circumscribed in terms of this antinomy. What alienates the subject is a system of transcendental hallucination and illusion that obviously goes unnoticed, but which the subject has to notice and whose spell he has to shake off, without being able simply to destroy it, in order to constitute himself as such or as subject *for* the world. To believe that the world can be treated in the same way as an object in the world, that it gives rise to the same kinds of illusion, would simply be a philosophical delusion. The proper distinction is not so much between world and entity as between the world supposedly subsisting in-itself (within an operational transcendence) and the world as reduced or delivered from its sufficiency. Consequently, the distinction is not so much between the world and another realm of practice in-itself, or between the world and a transcendent realm of practice, but between two ways of relating to the world, one governed by the world, the other determined-according-to-the-real. The heterogeneity between the subject-agency and the site of production is not traced from transcendence in general but rather articulated in terms of the kind of scission proper to determination-in-the-last-instance, which is the scission between a transcendence which is assumed to be in-itself and a transcendence-in-radical-immanence.

When we say that intervention does not operate upon the world, this is too vague and equivocal a formulation, since there is a sense in which the world is also employed for the auto-constitution of the subject. What we mean is that intervention does not operate 'upon (the illusion of) the world in-itself,' which is acknowledged but not destroyed. The hallucination and illusion continue to subsist for themselves: although they are acknowledged or identified, they continue to enjoy *for themselves* the capacity to re-engender the *absolute belief* in the world, a belief that persists as such. It is only for the subject that they are acknowledged and that the world can also be used or dismembered. The world is two faces in one: belief and pretension on the one hand, a material for constituting the subject on the other.

VII. An Immanent Practice against the Exception of Thought

One initial consequence of the foregoing considerations is that of the simultaneously objectivist and ideal character of action and its effects. Since philosophical thought is oriented toward transcendence, the structure of philosophy requires it to describe ideal or idealized situations and to legislate about the world in a detached, contemplative manner without implicating itself in its own discourse, or rather by exempting itself from it. Philosophical thought cumulates the negative effects of a mode of objectivity that is indifferent both to its objects and to its own re-absorption into a unitary circuit. This is a consequence of philosophical thought's tendency toward 'objectivation' and its pernicious mode of 'attachment' to the object; it follows from objectivation as a mode of objectivity that takes up a position of survey or overview relative to its object and ultimately evaporates into contemplation. Philosophy can only distinguish between enunciation and enunciability (which it conflates with the enunciated) or between objectivation and objectivity (which it conflates with the objectified) in a weak, unitary fashion—even more so perhaps than other forms of thought—that fails to constitute them as rigorously heterogeneous orders.

Although an explicit philosophy of practice seems to be free of this idealizing tendency and seems to take on board the gravity of action, by using the term 'practice' it too perpetuates the unitary conflation between ideal practical objectivity and action upon the world. It protects the former, which formulates the meaning and worth of things—what is good and bad, true or false for the world—from the latter. And with regard to itself, the philosophy of practice believes that it has achieved something sufficient but also something superior by setting out the aforementioned distinction, which makes of it an exception to the world and allows it to enunciate laws, norms and essences without itself falling under them, since it instantiates their 'higher' form. Philosophy begins by putting itself on the same level or plane as the world, but this is only so as to raise itself above it and present itself as the true and authentic form of science, art, truth, ethics, etc., in such a way as to end up turning itself into an exception and instituting its exception as the absolute that rules and consummates its own (seemingly democratic) primary combination with the world. If philosophy is intrinsically political, as is so often but so glibly maintained, it is intrinsically anti-democratic.

The entire theory of philosophy's practice, causality, effects and efficacy is vitiated by this exceptional status that philosophy ascribes to its own thought, by its ulterior motivation, its cunning which is not cunning, etc. Can we introduce seriousness and work into thought in place and instead of the pathos of seriousness and gravity which has made it so light-headed? Can we put practice into theory rather than just inserting practice 'in theory'? Can we, ultimately, turn the thought of commitment into a commitment of thought? We are obviously assuming that in this current context mere inversion would be useless (which is to say philosophical), and that this kind of operation should be supplanted by others capable of transforming philosophy....

Superficially, the problem consists in channelling philosophical effects upon the world into the realm of thought as such. For example: how can 'democracy' also be attributed to the thought that attributes it to social life? How can philosophical enunciation finally be rendered democratic rather than merely functioning as a universal instance of legitimation while exempting both itself and the philosopher? The spontaneous solution to this problem would be to say that thought should be affected by its object or affect itself with its object. But this would be to reiterate the philosophical circle as auto-affection and would merely invert philosophy's primacy over politics and democracy. Marx would have seen in such a move a typically philosophical contortion or 'somersault,' one that reinforces philosophy's dialectical games and dissolves practice, as well as the democracy that is supposed to accompany it, in the vicious circle whereby everything becomes philosophy insofar as philosophy is affected by everything. The principle governing such a somersault is quite simple. Philosophical dualities, in which one term invariably enjoys a supplement of alterity and unity relative to the other, can be inverted and overturned because of this supplement, so that democracy becomes disseminated into philosophy and vice versa but always to the ultimate benefit of philosophy.

The principle behind the non-philosophical solution consists in exploiting the power of identity (which is un-convertible) rather than the power of philosophical duality (which is convertible). In order to eliminate division, difference and their quasi-dialectical games, what must be given—but without an act of giving—is an identity that is performative, or better still, that is performed without an act of performance, and that thereby contains the identity of thought, on the one hand, and those practical consequences that thought habitually enunciates or programs for the world, on the other. Of course, such an identity cannot really 'contain' two apparently—or at least philosophically—opposed entities such as these. In other words, it will 'contain' them only 'in-the-last-instance,' not as real parts, which would divide identity once again. But identity must be the determination of the now transcendental identity of thought and practice as forever inseparable. Determination-in-the-last-instance and cloning ensure the radical interlocking of thought and practice. We will call 'unified theory' this transcendental but determined identity of thought and practice, of knowledge and the consequences of action, which have now been withdrawn from the law of the world and the exception of philosophy. And we will require of every enterprise which claims to be non-philosophical that it take charge of, rather than merely internalize conceptually, all those effects and ideals it presumes to impose upon the world or what it calls the world.

Thus, the dilemma of theory and practice is resolved in a determination- or *performation-in-the-last-instance* (rather than the performativity traced from its linguistic form) of theory as practice. Moreover, the universality of practice is not tied to the specific positivity of its cause, which is without-consistency. Practice finds its freedom and universality not in nothingness (which no doubt would already suffice to liberate it) but in man-in-person as without-consistency.

VIII. Can We Intervene in the World?

The question of the political (or ethical) consequences of non-philosophy is usually badly formulated because it is formulated philosophically. Whenever it tries to think practice, philosophy postulates that it is possible to intervene in the world—'intervene' as philosophy understands it, obviously. What does such intervention mean when it applies to non-philosophy? Can an operation of the philosophical type apply only to things of the world?

Philosophy supposes, rightly or wrongly, that it has effects upon reality and it expects the same of non-philosophy. Wrongly perhaps, because what philosophy calls 'reality' is in any case a concept—attenuated at worst, elaborate at best—of the world. Through this concept, philosophy projects *a reality in-itself, which is to say, one that has been constructed in the realm of operational transcendence*, within which it claims to intervene, and in terms of which it gauges all possible intervention. But the real content of philosophy, once the illusion of the in-itself has been bracketed, is this very correlation between itself and the world. In any case, it is within *this* experience that non-philosophy can 'intervene,' and not in the philosophical concept of experience itself (which is too narrow and devised too much in the manner of a projection). We can universalize Kant's distinction between judgments of perception and judgments of experience and posit that our object is no longer the judgment of perception, whose role the philosophy of reality now plays for us, but the judgment of experience, i.e. the affirmation of existence as such, in terms of which philosophy-in-person, or philosophy as form of the world, presents itself. Philosophical intervention is itself highly problematic within the confines of a reality that is alternately anticipated and projected, forgotten and desired; it is both ahead of and lagging behind the conjuncture, 'in the midst of' experience and its combinations but without getting to grips with the identity of the conjuncture, whose significance escapes it.

Philosophy projects its operation of division and re-appropriation onto a diverse variety of things, objects and sensations through the intermediary of a schema which seems to be primarily derived from language and, in the order of so-called regional forms of knowledge, science. The latter provides it with forms of knowledge that philosophy abstracts from their process of production and which it uses to fill out its own universal, necessary structures, which combine difference and identity but are empty and so have to be filled. Thus, philosophy grafts itself onto experience and claims to intervene within it on the basis of an identification and confusion of the very orders it requires. Philosophy is a long-suffering desire for the real, to which it aspires but only so as to be able to construct or reaffirm itself in its own proper, consistent order—an order structured by those transcendentals which function like an absolute metaphor for experience.

Every intervention in philosophy, which is to say, every intervention upon its objects, remains intra-philosophical, caught up in philosophy's self-encompassing structure. Every such intervention, consequently, remains in the world. But insofar as every practice of this type remains subsumed beneath the law of self-positioning and its pretensions, so then (*from the point of view of non-philosophy*) it continues to postulate a philosophy or a world 'in-itself.' The world as in-itself or self-encompassing is the source of antinomies that only non-philosophy can identify and suspend.

Given these conditions, it is difficult to maintain that philosophy *transforms* the world. It *is* the world or attaches itself to regional representations as the very 'dimension' of the world. It 'transforms' regional representations in an ideal-real or representational (in the enlarged sense we have given this term) modality, regional representations that it appropriates and from which it extracts a surplus-value of meaning and empirical (but also transcendental or transformed empirical) content. Philosophical intervention consists in adding and subtracting philosophy, as the form of the world, to and from things. It consists in interpretation.

So what can non-philosophy hope to achieve with regard to the world itself? The non-philosophical operation is quite different from the philosophical version: it no longer comprises the combination of division and identity but instead radical identity and hence unilateral duality. The result is a gain in simplicity and minimality. Non-philosophy does not project itself onto things but solicits them necessarily and says so without trying to hide the fact in the manner that philosophy sometimes does. On the other hand, it clones subjects from philosophy, and here again cloning is the reduced or minimal form, the real core of philosophical projection. As for its object, this is now the world or the philosophy-form as such, rather than things. Consequently, non-philosophy is not an intensified reduplication of philosophy, a meta-philosophy, but rather its 'simplification.' It does not represent a change in scale with respect to philosophy, as though the structure of the latter were maintained for smaller elements. It is the 'same' structure but in a more concentrated, more focused form—it is withdrawn from identity as merely desired and brought to the level of identity as performed. It is a non-unity rather than a meta-unity. The gesture is one of universalization, of simplification in the number of postulates. This simplification, which is achieved through the suspension of a certain postulate (that of the reciprocal determination of thought and the real), is capable of producing an explanation of philosophy *insofar as it can be explained and in the terms in which it can.* As in philosophy, there is a practical gain at the level of theory, but a theory that is wholly different from the philosophical kind.

IX. Interpretation, Transformation, Determination-in-the-Last-Instance

How does all this affect the duality of interpretation and transformation (Marx) once this duality has been reconceived according to the primacy of practice, and once practice has been prized free from philosophical difference and determined-according-to-the-real? Philosophy is interpretation at a global level because it is infinite repetition and self-reference, overview and contemplation of the world in the narrow sense presupposed by philosophy. Yet it also comprises a transcendental recursion, relating through itself to experience, which it does not so much dominate in the manner of a transcendent religious heaven as 'transform' or help 'constitute.' But is constitution equivalent to transformation as defined by an immanent performative practice?

Philosophy, as we have already observed, is not wholly devoid of operations, but these operations—such as overturning and displacement, to say nothing of more specular ones such as hermeneutics, or auto-specular ones such as the dialectic—not only operate at the heart of representations, they also operate with these representations: combining them, analyzing them, deconstructing them, dialecticizing them. Philosophy programs a transformation of the world, but one which is ideal, objectified, incapable of getting an effective grip on it; one that achieves something akin to an effect only by adding to or subtracting from what is given (conceived now as a representation) new and equally ideal determinations that double and then redouble it, simplifying or even deconstructing it without really transforming it. Throughout its practice, twentieth-century philosophy has admitted and shown—but only ever under its breath, so to speak, without ever 'truly' being aware of it (thereby demonstrating the extent to which its practice remains ideal)—that it has only ever worked with representations, with the logos, which is to say with metaphysics, even as it tried to criticize or deconstruct the latter. Such philosophy remains under the jurisdiction of philosophical tradition and submits to the authority of its tribunal. *Genuine transformation does not consist in playing a game (whether at the level of language, of practice, or of the world) with representation, but rather in determining the latter through a radically un-representable agency or instance—more precisely, through a without-representation that allows itself to be thought by means of representations which have been reduced to the status of philosophically inert material.*

Since the world has now been enlarged to include all possible philosophical thought, it is likewise necessary to enlarge the concept of representation and relate it to an agency or instance that has to function like a 'last instance' for it, rather than an 'ulterior instance,' a world-behind-the-scenes or thing-in-itself. Every instance of thought that is left to itself and not determined by a without-representation-of-the-last-instance is a representation in this widened sense of the term. To put it another way: we will call 'representation' every presentation that refers back to itself through a transcendental recursion that, although capable of criticizing, deconstructing or modifying presentation, cannot determine-it-in-(the)-real.

As for non-philosophy, it uses these representations, which are by definition its only material, but so as to confer upon them a new condition relative to their philosophical condition as *combinations*. We call this new condition a 'mixture' because it is the transcendental identity of a duality of philosophical representations and (for example) scientific or artistic operations that are delivered from their subsumption by philosophy. This is a duality without an operation of synthesis or analysis.

X. A Transcendental Practice

A genuinely transformative practice must answer to several conditions. Among other things, it must be genuinely practical, which is to say, *real by virtue of its cause*, in order not to become confused with globally ideal representations. It must also be capable of relating immanently or transcendentally, rather than externally or in an empirico-idealist fashion, to these representations. It is often and erroneously imagined that practice is opposed to idealism but above all opposed to philosophy's transcendental dimension. This is because philosophy lives off those divisions and hierarchies through which primacy and priority are linked together, and because the transcendental approach has traditionally been idealist, whereas it is in fact that aspect of the real which is 'other than…'

Consequently, it is the philosophical apparatus as a whole which must be completely overhauled, practically transformed, so as to give back to practice its immanent force. Once the transcendental is determined by the real, as is the case in non-philosophy, it changes its status, it no longer represents the apex of an ontological hierarchy but rather a function which the real may or may not assume. Since practice is indissociable from the syntax of unilateral duality that follows from the real, it is indissociable from the real's transcendental function. Practical effects and transcendental function are identical for the real; they are possible functions of it that become effectuated once the world is taken into account for itself or solicits the real and the latter 'responds' to that solicitation—on account of the world's being-given-in-the-real—with a transcendental practice.

Far from being a crude primary activity, or an idealist activity taken from the world (as is the case, for philosophical reasons, with Fichte), practice is the transcendental essence of the subject insofar as the latter is now distinguished from the world, which the subject uses as an occasion or material. This is why practice consists in transforming or dualyzing representations and ceases to be an 'activity' grafted onto these representations and controlling them both from within and from without. Practice is transcendental through its real immanent root, which renders it radically heterogeneous to all representation. But this heterogeneity does not prevent it from being transcendental or effectuated by those representations that make up the world. Like the real, practice is immanent, but there is nothing to prevent it from relating to representations or from being sufficiently heterogeneous to these representations to be able to transform them. Obviously, in spite of its origin in the real, the transcendental is not valid for supposedly absolute representations or for the world insofar as it is supposed to be in-itself, but only for the world-form or for the philosophy-form as a priori form of the world. Like practice, the transcendental pertains to this a priori form rather than to objects or to the world-object as sufficient reality.

XI. The Pragmatic Appropriation of Philosophy

"Man is universally predestined to philosophy just as philosophy has man as its destination"—this is the fundamental postulate of philosophy: that philosophy and man are reciprocally convertible on condition of a certain labor, education or ascesis. In order to render this postulate credible, in order to put it into practice and ensure its dominion over man, philosophy claims to define man by means of some circular duality (e.g. as a rational, linguistic or religious animal), a duality that is ultimately unitary and encompassing (man as the metaphysical animal). This begs the question by simply presupposing an interface between philosophy and man in the form of his philosophical definition, which is always an exclusive, unitary definition. It is a package deal: a definition of man is possible provided it is philosophical and posits the convertibility between a putative human essence and its attributes. 'Man' becomes a combination of all sorts of essences and properties, depending on the doctrine in question: a generality in which what should have been distinguished non-philosophically—man's non-philosophical essence—is instead conflated with an infinitely nuanced definition that encapsulates an entire philosophical system. In order to think man, or to think him in a manner adequate to his being, a distinction must cut across 'man' as generality. But in order to avoid begging the question and so as to render the distinction rigorous, it should no longer coincide with any of those philosophical 'differences' (of degree, kind, form, writing, affect or will). We will leave behind these aporias and the politics of the philosophical subjection of humans by positing the following axioms:

1. 'Man,' 'ego,' 'subject,' 'human(s)' are no longer concepts but primary names posed in axioms.
2. Primary names are terms extracted from philosophy but abstracted from their naïve intuitive horizon, from the world of metaphysical objects and representations. Their signifying base serves as a support for an alternative logic, an alternative organization of thought which we will call 'non-philosophy.'
3. Non-philosophical thought and its theoretical practice are determined by its object, which we will designate by the symbol 'man-in-man' ('in-man' for short, or even 'man' when the context precludes misunderstanding). Such thought is not derived or received from some ex-

ternal or philosophical source, and it has the power to abstract philosophical terms from the realm of meaning within which they normally function.

4. The 'object' of non-philosophy, and that which determines it, is its cause: 'man-in-man.'
5. Man-in-man is not a concept or unitary entity. It is not amenable to definition: it is posited through real-transcendental axioms.

Posited in this way, the human is no longer a unitary generality, a conflation of the concept with the real object, of the attribute with the 'essence.' On the one hand, this is the *in-man* as real rather than ideal cause, as the real rather than a reason or even the principle of reason. On the other hand, this is a *subject* in a new sense because the real is no longer the absolute subject of philosophy or even the classical subject; it is now ascribed to the in-man alone. The subject is no longer the real or something that cooperates with the real but rather an operation exercised upon the world or upon philosophy and constituting itself through that exercise. But the relation to the world and the supposedly essential relation to philosophy are no longer attributed to the human cause. For the expression 'man-in-man' means that the latter is without a determining essence, without consistency; dispossessed of nothingness as much as being, dispossessed of substance as much as presence-to-itself. Of course this distinction is no longer a difference, which is to say a unitary structure, a more or less asymmetrical convertibility between cause and subject. The latter are *radically but not absolutely* distinct. The in-man is radically autonomous because man can only be found in-man rather than in philosophy or the world. But the subject is in an altogether more complex and more interesting situation. It is not between the in-man and the world, as though it constituted their (once more divided) in-between or their difference, or a duality of two substances. It is the *indivisible clone* produced on the basis of the world under the influence of the in-man. This is not some new version of man as the microcosm who is convertible with the macrocosm, give or take a difference in scale. The subject registers the minimum of relationality that philosophy imposes upon the in-man but also the clone-form that the latter imposes upon philosophy. Yet although they are the asymmetrical cooperation of distinct roles, the cause and the subject are not juxtaposed. Since man and the subject are identical in-man or in-the-last-instance, the subject enjoys a relative autonomy which he gains from that of philosophy so that he is not entirely indistinguishable from the in-man. We say that he is determined-in-the-last-instance by the in-man.

Insofar as he is posited in this 'ultimate' fashion through a theoretical act we call a 'primary ultimation,' man no longer has a privileged or essential affinity with philosophy. Instead, he receives it as a realm of (no doubt 'fundamental') objects, as the universal and necessary form of the world. Non-philosophy proposes to examine the fundamental structures of this a priori world-form while at the same time using it with a view to providing its theoretical explanation. Man is no longer a concept or even the object of a concept and, being devoid of essence, he cannot be *essentially* destined to a philosophical activity which now interests him only in the context of a practice in which he is a *subject-for-philosophy*. Humans are without-philosophy—not just men without qualities but men who are primarily without essence, yet all the more *destined-for-the-world or philosophy without having decided or willed it.* Philosophy has always wanted us and we have been obliged to consent to it—but have we ever wanted philosophy?

The critique of the philosophical 'end' of philosophy and of its sufficiency in foreseeing and deciding its own death leads back to man-in-person, not to man insofar as he is capable of lack of interest, lack of purpose, or indifference. This is not a void that one describes in the hope of shoring up by returning to or reactivating a past of which we have been disinherited. We call 'appropriation of philosophy' the theory of philosophy carried out on the basis of the real-transcendental indifference that philosophy itself effectuates. What is radically poor in essence and in philosophy remains radically poor throughout this appropriation whereby philosophy is cloned as what is proper to man-in-person. Appropriation has none of the bulimic or anorexic traits of re-appropriation: it is what is poor in philosophy as such that takes the latter into consideration and strips it of its sufficiency. It is by virtue of this poverty that the human relation to philosophy takes the form of a pragmatics determined-in-the-last-instance rather than an auto-pragmatics. To abandon the end of philosophy to metaphysics alone, to repeat the gesture of self-positing in a nihilist mode and turn it into a gesture of self-repudiation, is to fail to see that this end still harbors a sense-of-the-last-instance for man-in-man—but this is precisely a non-philosophical or *other than*... philosophical sense. With the end of philosophy, it becomes easier to see the extent to which philosophy exerts its 'grip' on the radical human subject. Consequently, the hypothesis of men-without-philosophy means that the latter is not an attribute and that our transcendental and contingent relation to it is brought forth with man-in-person and effectuated by philosophy itself as material [*comme matériau*]. It is a question of restoring or rather giving to philosophy a utopian and u-chronic force that it has deprived itself of—or that it has been deprived of as a result of man-in-person's being-foreclosed.

Non-philosophy is a program for appropriating philosophy itself as necessary relation to the world, since our 'experience' is the world as such. Non-philosophical cognition does not relate to the world as an entity or to entities in the world (as objects or forms of knowledge): it is transcendental and exposes the reality of a cognition that relates to philosophy as the world's a priori form, as 'knowledge' or 'existence' of the world.

Afterword

Theology and Non-Philosophy

Laruelle's recent work has attempted to theorize the life of the non-philosophical Stranger-subject, a life which, though it cannot be subjective or human in an essential sense, must be distinguished from the real One that it posits. Whereas the immanent real is in-man or in-person, the non-philosophical subject posits this immanence and lives in and through this positing. The life of the subject is, according to Laruelle, a *faithful* adherence to generic scientific or theoretical procedures—an adherence to the axiom of an immanent identity that is foreclosed from the world, and to the theorems that follow from this axiom. The subject lives in the faithful application of these procedures to philosophical material and also, as in some of Laruelle's most recent work, to religious material.[1] The non-philosophical or non-religious subject lives *only* in this application. Arriving as if from nowhere, from no time or place apart from the world as it is, the Stranger-subject pos-

1. See especially *Le Christ futur: un lecon d'heresie* (Paris: Exils, 2002). This book has recently been published in English translation as *Future Christ: A Lesson in Heresy*, tr. Anthony Paul Smith (London and New York: Continuum, 2011). Laruelle extends this work, especially as it concerns the relation of belief and faith, in the essay "A Science in Christ," tr. Aaron Riches, in *The Grandeur of Reason: Religion, Tradition and Universalism*, eds. Peter Candler, Jr. and Conor Cunningham (Canterbury: SCM, 2010). Here Laruelle specifically discusses the generic functioning of Christ's axiomatic language.

its the vision-in-One only by suspending the reciprocal mediation of immanence and transcendence in worldly thought. The life of the subject depends for its occasion on the various forms of philosophical and religious thought that are structured by the presumption of a transcendental that determines (and is determined by) the realm of the immanent given.

Faith-in-Life: Future-Christ

In the case of religion, the suspension of mediation preempts belief in a divine source of the visible world. This suspension differs from the dogmatic assertions of atheists, who insist that they know and possess the transcendent as a reified nothing. The application of non-philosophical procedures to religious materials requires a subject who is non-Christian and also non-atheist, a subject for whom transcendence is not negated but suspended by being posited as ultimately identical, without synthesis, to what appears as immanent to worldly thought. This ultimate identity is the immanence of-the-last-instance, the immanence of the One in which the mutually-determining immanence and transcendence of philosophy are together given-without-givenness.

The figure of Christ has, for Laruelle, become the model of the non-religious suspension of reciprocal mediation, for the most scandalous statements of Christ were and remain the axiomatic assertions by which he assumed identity with divine law and logos, the two principles of mediation that structured the order of his world. By identifying these structures in himself, in his own flesh, Christ called them radically into question: to *be* the logos as such is necessarily to present the source of this divine word; and to *be* the law is to embody a perfection that law as such can only indicate. Thus in Christ the transcendent does not somehow *become* immanent; rather his axioms suspend their mutual relation according to a more ultimate identity. In claiming to be these principles of mediation, Christ seems to assert that there is nothing any longer to mediate. With the perfection of mediation announced by Christ, the transcendent realm, along with the law and logos that had upheld it, is nowhere but in-him—that is to say, in Laruelle's terms, in the radical immanence, the identity-of-the-last-instance, of his positing.

Laruelle calls his account of Christ's action non-Christian because the suspension of mediation leaves nothing in which to *believe*. The notion of belief presupposes a philosophical mode of knowledge in which the divine gives and is discerned through the world; belief in divinity becomes a way of knowing the object and content of faith. Laruelle suggests that there is a more radical, non-religious faith—a faith adhering to the generic non-philosophical axioms that suspend mediation and produce the world as given-without-givenness, as given beyond any possible philosophical retrieval of the giving.

The suspension of mediation is itself immediately and unaccountably given in the postulation of immanent identity—and this postulation is in-the-last-instance identical to the materials of mediated worldly knowledge that function as its occasion. The positing of the One cannot be induced from any worldly phenomena, nor can it be deduced from any prior suppositions. According only with the unknowable immanent identity of the real, this axiom announces an "unlearned knowledge" (a phrase that Laruelle uses to allude to the disembodied intuitions of gnosis). And because this "knowledge" cannot be derived and lacks any form of its own, it requires faith to effectuate it, to bring it to life in this world.

The positing of the ultimate identity of the One is empty and meaningless apart from the structures of worldly knowing that it neutralizes and suspends. The articulation of the vision-in-One occurs only in the faithfully asserted identity-without-synthesis of particular determinations of immanence and transcendence, of objectivity and its philosophical derivation. The vision-in-One must therefore be posited or effectuated again and again, always through its neutralization, without negation, of particular hierarchical structures of worldly knowledge. The faith of Christ, according to Laruelle, lives only in his asserted identity to law and logos, an identity that suspends these mediating principles of worldly order, and thereby brings forth their world as identical in-the-last-instance to an immanence that they cannot know or master. And Christ must live again—the living faith of a "future Christ" is always required—because philosophical knowledge perpetually attempts to objectify and transcend the radical immanence to which it is nonetheless identical. This is the immanence of the future itself, a future that is always identical to what has already been given, insofar as this given is radically inconsistent with the predictable motions of philosophical attenuation and objectification.

The subject that lives into this future, the Stranger-subject or future Christ, is a non-individual, non-egoistic subject deprived of concrete form in the world. The subject arrives from and disappears into the future that he opens by positing the ultimate identity of every worldly form in an immanence that remains unknown and undetermined. In the present the subject lives in the application of axioms to the worldly structures he suspends. His life is an impersonal faith in this application and suspension, in generic non-philosophical functions and the immanent future to which they are committed. There is no object to this faith-without-belief. It is a lived adherence to the efficacy of the unlearned or axiomatic knowledge of ultimate identity. To adhere to these axioms requires faith because they have no knowable efficacy: the suspension of mediation accomplishes nothing within the world; rather it exposes the world as a whole to the future, which is nothing other than the immanence that cannot be known and objectified by predictable philosophical transformations.

The fidelity of the Christ-subject to the immanent future that he posits is also, according to Laruelle, his fidelity to all of those whose violent exclusion from the world ensures that they live in an immemorial and unforgettable past. In the vision-in-One everything other than or excluded from the world is seen as nonetheless identical to the world in-the-last-instance. The unknown past, the past of the nameless victims, and the unknown future, unilaterally exposed, are One with the world in the ultimate real. By living according to the positing of this ultimate identity, by effecting the neutralization of the worldly order founded on the denial of this identity, the Christ-subject shares the immanent life of past and future, of victim and redeemer.

Belief and Faith: Theological Questions

Laruelle's focus on the figure of the "future Christ," and his more recent engagement with Christian mysticism in still untranslated works[2], have raised questions as to the precise relation between the discourses of non-philosophy and Christian theology. Though the preemption of belief by an immediate and objectless faith is supposed to separate non-Christianity from the Christian tradition, this preemption may be based on a simplified understanding of traditional belief as directed towards a presupposed transcendent source of given objectivity. For the ban on idolatry, the first axiom of monotheistic religion,

2. *Mystique non-philosophique à l'usage des contemporains* [*Non-Philosophical Mysticism for Contemporary Use*] (Paris: L'Harmattan, 2007).

calls into question all presupposed notions of knowable divinity. God as *creator* cannot be known as the conditioning source of the world, as if he were a First Cause or Primal Being without qualitative difference from finite beings and causes. God cannot be known as the cause of any discernible effect.[3] The transcendence of the creator can be known only insofar as it is paradoxically immanent in and as the world it creates and sustains. Indeed one can understand the divine act of creation as a cause of-the-last-instance, a cause that applies to everything, but only insofar as it is seen according to the Oneness of God's ultimate and ungraspable reality—a real immanence identical to but radically inconsistent with the world as it appears. The faith that adheres to the non-philosophical vision-in-One, that takes everything in the world as given-without-givenness, is perhaps closer than Laruelle realizes to trust in an unknown God, a trust that allows for the world in all its diversity and inconsistency to be received as a single unfathomable *gift*.

If, however, the objectless character of traditional and non-idolatrous belief can seem to resemble non-religious faith, the converse may also hold true: Laruelle's ostensibly objectless faith may not, despite his efforts, be entirely purged of a positive content. Belief and faith are not easily dualyzed, not only because the ban on idolatry has already (non-religiously) fore-

3. Etienne Gilson, commenting on a passage from Aquinas' *De Potentia* (q. 3, a. 1), says that "creation is not a change, because to create is not to make something from something else…" See Gilson, *The Elements of Christian Philosophy* (New York: Doubleday, 1960), 193. Herbert McCabe, OP, following Gilson, pointedly summarizes the relevant implications of the classical doctrine: "…creation does not make any *difference* to anything, it is not a matter of a transition from one kind of thing to another kind of thing…. In thinking of something as *creature* we are not thinking of it in contrast and distinction from other creatures, we are thinking of it, or trying to think of it, as existing instead of not existing." See Herbert McCabe, *God Matters* (London and New York: Continuum, 1987), 150.

closed transcendence from the realm of objective and worldly thought, but also because faith, in Laruelle's own account, is ambiguously tied to the worldly and historical figure of Jesus Christ. This tie seems to contradict Laruelle's own understanding of faith as adherence to a world-less "unlearned knowledge." The fidelity of Christ, Laruelle contends, is not specific to him personally: indeed Christ's own individual personality is neutralized in the way he lives according to the postulation of the immanent identity of every worldly thing (including himself). This fidelity need not be tied to the worldly image of Christ because it is impersonal and can therefore be lived in every subject whose place in the world is called into question by the positing of radical immanence. According to Laruelle, the faith of Christ lives not in the visible acts that characterize his personal and worldly image, but in his axiomatic suspension of mediation, in his self-identification as law and logos. The 'self' thus identified exists nowhere except in its positing and in the identity that it effects. Christ cannot exist without the law and logos that he neutralizes, and that is why the future Christ is always required: non-religious axioms must be similarly applied to other regimes of mediation and worldly order.

But why, if faith is the life adhering to generic non-philosophical procedure, does Laruelle focus on the figure of Christ? Why does Laruelle invoke *this* name? The answer cannot be, as Laruelle sometimes suggests, that he is simply making non-religious use of given religious and theological material. The future Christ is not simply cloned from the image of Christ that appears in this world. For as Laruelle also makes clear, the axioms of Christ, his asserted identity to law and logos, are the model for the non-philosophical and non-religious positing of radical immanence—to the extent that Laruelle's proposed generic science of religion would be a "science in Christ." And these axioms cannot be entirely separated from the worldly figure of Christ (which is worldly simply insofar as it appears, regardless of how this appearance is understood, whether as historical or mythological or in some other way). Does not Laruelle imply the indispensability of this figure, if only by his fidelity to the name?

Even if the significance of Christ lies in his adherence to impersonal and generic scientific procedures, one must still ask about the relation between the worldly Christ and the positing of world-less "unlearned knowledge" that has been associated with him. If there is *any* relation, if Christ is not simply an arbitrary name for the life of generic scientific procedures that can arrive anytime and anywhere, inexplicably and without condition, then the figure of Christ takes on an exceptional *eminence*—in other words, transcendence—that threatens the finality of the immanence he ostensibly posits. If the worldly Christ, the figure that has arisen and taken its place in worldly history, is in some way *necessary* for the positing of the identity of radical immanence, then Christ simply cannot be identical in-the-last-instance to this supposedly ultimate reality. It seems that Laruelle's ostensibly generic Christ-subject, standing *out* from the One that he posits, introduces an ineluctable transcendence into the heart of the immanent One.[4]

Non-philosophy dualyzes immanence and transcendence by positing them as in-the-last-instance identical in radical immanence. For theology, by contrast, immanence and transcendence are neither distinguishable nor identical: they cannot be differentially related in philosophical fashion, as if they were

4. In his most recent work, much of it still unpublished, Laruelle takes up these questions and proposes a unilateral complementarity between Christ, understood as generic Messianic life, and the actual Jesus, understood as Christ's historical "occasion."

two objects; but neither can they be identified according to the non-philosophical axiom that the ultimate and unknowable transcendental for worldly thought is radical immanence. Instead theology takes transcendence as *itself immanent*, as itself given-without-givenness in a world of things that are simultaneously interrelated and incommensurable. Transcendence is internal to the structure of things that exist in mutually determining relation to each other, a relation that is *positive* and not just differential or dialectical; and so transcendence cannot, even in-the-last-instance, be foreclosed from any form of worldly knowledge. Transcendence *as such* is foreclosed: that which gives the world as a whole is as unknowable for theology as it is for non-philosophy; the doctrine of creation insists that the world is given without a philosophically recoverable givenness. But this doctrine also implies that human beings assert their belief in an ultimate transcendence simply by perceiving the world in all its beauty and diversity—a perception which requires that they attend to some worldly objects more than to others, granting them relative eminence.

To attend to the world in this way, to receive it as constituted and held together in its very being by the mutual determination of incommensurable forms, is to believe in the living reality of transcendence-in-immanence. It is to receive the world as dynamically structured at its deepest level by an incarnate mystery. For there is an inescapably positive and *creative* aspect of causal interrelationships, even at the worldly level. Of course causes can always be philosophically derived as conditioning their effects (and vice-versa, in the movement of reciprocal determination). But philosophy can never use causes and effects to account exhaustively for each other; what remains mysterious is the separation, the shared discretion, of causal factors from their effects—which nonetheless shape and affect each other. In this separation is the unaccountable creative power of causality, by which interrelated worldly elements *give being* to each other by giving each other the space freely and distinctly to be, while still remaining always in mutually constitutive relation. To accept the reality of things is to believe in the immanence of this ultimately transcendent power.[5]

For theology, then, some form of belief inheres in the life of the subject—even the non-philosophical one. The preemption of belief by generic faith threatens to harden into an untenable distinction. Though vulnerable to all sorts of worldly and philosophical abuses, belief in a truly transcendent being—given the strictures of monotheistic revelation, beginning with the ban on idolatry—cannot be philosophical in Laruelle's sense. There is in the very notion of ultimate transcendence a built-in check on the philosophical manipulations that would capture it for worldly knowledge. And conversely, faith cannot be truly world-less and imageless. The images and objects of faith must be provisional, broken in advance by ultimate transcendence; but there can be no primal trust or faith without visible forms to elicit it and bring it to life. Could Laruelle have articulated his non-religious faith without the direction provided by his

5. See again Gilson, who notes Aquinas' statements in *De Potentia* (q. 7, a. 2): "All the created causes communicate in one effect, which is being, although everyone of them has its proper effect, and this distinguishes it from the others....There must therefore be a cause higher than all the causes, a cause because of which they themselves cause being..." At the basis of all causal efficacy, says Gilson in interpreting Aquinas, is the power of the cause to communicate its being to the effect; this communication occurs as the cause gives its own separate form to the effect, a separation which is not a difference but a sharing of common being. Creation, says Gilson, "is the prototype of causal efficiency, and if they are to be conceived as contributing to the very being of their effects, finite beings are efficient causes only inasmuch as, in acting, they imitate the first efficient act, cause of all other beings as well as of their causal fecundity." Gilson, *The Elements of Christian Philosophy*, 206-7.

personal belief in—his inclination towards, his attention to, his imagination of—Jesus Christ?

Gabriel Alkon, Boris Gunjevic
April 2011

Also from Telos Press

Jens-Martin Eriksen & Frederik Stjernfelt
The Democratic Contradictions of Multiculturalism

Timothy W. Luke and Ben Agger
A Journal of No Illusions
Telos, *Paul Piccone, and the Americanization of Critical Theory*

Carl Schmitt
Hamlet or Hecuba: The Intrusion of the Time into the Play

Victor Zaslavsky
Class Cleansing: The Massacre at Katyn

Ernst Jünger
On Pain

Paul Piccone
Confronting the Crisis: Writings of Paul Piccone

Matthias Küntzel
Jihad and Jew-Hatred: Islamism, Nazism, and the Roots of 9/11

Carl Schmitt
Theory of the Partisan